Girls Seen and Heard

Preface by Carol Gilligan, Ph.D.,

and Marie C. Wilson, M.S.

■

Jeremy P. Tarcher/Putnam

a member of Penguin Putnam Inc.

New York

Girls Seen and Heard

52 Life Lessons for Our Daughters

Ms. Foundation for Women

Creator of Take Our Daughters to Work® Day

and Sondra Forsyth

Identifying information and names of individuals have been changed in some cases.

Most Tarcher/Putnam books are available at special quantity discounts for bulk purchases for sales promotions, premiums, fund-raising, and educational needs. Special books or book excerpts also can be created to fit specific needs. For details, write or telephone Putnam Special Markets, 200 Madison Avenue, New York, NY 10016; (212) 951-8891.

Jeremy P. Tarcher/Putnam
a member of
Penguin Putnam Inc.
200 Madison Avenue
New York, NY 10016
www.penguinputnam.com

Library of Congress Cataloging-in-Publication Data
Forsyth, Sondra.
Girls seen and heard : 52 life lessons for our daughters / by Ms. Foundation . . .
and Sondra Forsyth ; preface by Carol Gilligan and Marie C. Wilson.
p.   cm.
ISBN 0-87477-926-X
1. Mothers and daughters. 2. Daughters—Psychology. 3. Teenage girls—
Psychology. 4. Sex role. 5. Self-esteem in adolescence. 6. Parenting. 7. Parents—
Conduct of life. I. Ms. Foundation for Women (U.S.). II. Title.
HQ755.85.F687   1998   97-52667 CIP
306.874'3—dc21

Book design by Chris Welch
Cover design by Kiley Thompson
Cover photo and interior frontispiece © by Mark Wagoner/Picturesque

Printed in the United States of America
10   9   8   7   6   5   4   3   2   1

This book is printed on acid-free paper. ♾

Acknowledgments

This book could not have come into existence without the bright mind, strong spirit, and just plain hard work of Heidi Burbage, program organizer at the Ms. Foundation for Women. She did extensive research for this project. Even more important, however, she contributed insights and ideas based on her solid knowledge of social and gender issues. Our profound thanks to her for a job not only well done, but done beyond the call of duty.

Our deep appreciation also goes to Melissa Silverstein, chief of staff of the Ms. Foundation for Women, who was at the ready to field questions, solve problems, and make sure the process of getting the book in shape for publication went smoothly. She also proved to be a sharp-eyed copyeditor, catching every spelling error and misplaced comma before the manuscript went to the publisher.

We would like to thank everyone at Tarcher/Putnam, in particular Jocelyn Wright and the entire production team.

Loretta Barrett, our literary agent, is one of a kind. She brings to her work more than twenty years of experience as a top editor at Doubleday, and that—coupled with her fine business sense—makes her an invaluable ally. She is also wise, witty, spiritual, and fun. We are privileged to have her represent us.

The lessons you are about to read come from the hard work of many individuals. Take Our Daughters to Work® Day is possible because of the people who have dedicated countless hours to making sure that millions of girls go to work each year. First and foremost, communications consultant Nell Merlino, who took two years' worth of our applied research and made it into a workable idea; Gail Maynor, whose love for the program and for girls has kept it working; Jill Savitt, Lauren Wechsler, and Melissa Silverstein, who spent hours carrying it to the next steps; and Kristen Golden, Tara Tremmel, Miriam Zoll, Elliot Thomson, Colleen McCabe, and Heidi Burbage, who created major pieces of the work as they did it. Most of the people who work on this program each year do so on a volunteer basis, far away from the Ms. Foundation's base of operations. We are particularly indebted to our "network of organizers," which continues to grow and flourish, and to our colleagues at Girl Scouts of the USA, Girls Inc., YWCA, AAUW, and other organizations working to improve girls' lives.

And to the others whose contribution has been significant in making it possible for girls to be *seen* and *heard*: Carolyn and George McKecuen, Debbie Merrill and her colleagues at McKecuen Consulting Inc., Watermark Association of Artisans, Elise Newman, Brigette Rouson, Carla Lovas, Sara Gould, Tanya Selvaratnam, Judy Schoenberg, Lisa Sjostrum, Redina Jackson, Gingi Pica, Idelisse Malave, Jodi Grossblatt, Adrena Ifill, Hildy Karp, Diane Paylor, Jackie Gelman, Beth Scully, Bette Yee, Carol Perline, Kathy Streiter, Elizabeth Debold, Janet Andre, Lisa Buksbaum, Helen Ross, Amy Schottenfeld, Pat Martin, Keith Thomson, Jasmine Victoria, Presley Edwards, Sandra Garcia, Kathy Gates, Linda Gates, Shawn White, Hanna Steffian, Jim Levine, Todd Pitinsky, Barnie Brawer, Alan Creighton, and the Oakland Men's Project.

Take Our Daughters to Work® Day would not have been possible without the support of key corporate leaders and friends: Walter Anderson, Pat Carbine, Al Dietzel, Phil Donahue, Linda Ellerbee, Alan Gabbay, Harry Hohn, Carol Jenkins, Lanny Jones, Doug McCormick, Ann Moore, Carol Reuter, Gloria Steinem, Arthur Sulzberger, Jr., Marlo Thomas, Jane Tollinger, Meredith Wagner, and Nancy Walker.

This book is dedicated to the millions of women and men who saw
Take Our Daughters to Work® Day as an opportunity to
change the lives of our nation's daughters. . . . It has.

For my sensitive and assertive son, Christopher
For my assertive and sensitive daughter, Stacey
And for all of "my kids," especially Alice, Alicia, Arman, Carson,
Drew, Eve, Hope, Janet, Jennifer, Jessica, Lisa-Brett, Margot,
Nora, Peggy, Raeman, Randy, Raymond, Sana Ali,
Scott, and Solomon

—S.F.

And for all of our daughters and sons

Contents

Part Two: Explore Your Options

Part Three: Command Respect

Appendix: Reader's Guide

Preface

We never set out to create Take Our Daughters to Work day—or anything like it. We began our work on girls just as we begin our work on every issue—by reviewing and discussing what activists and researchers were doing in the field and developing a plan to respond to it.

A great deal of information about the research on girls appears on the following pages, and we won't restate it here; a quick shorthand of the findings that had come out of Harvard University and other places in the early 1990s was "confident at 11, confused at 16," as a *New York Times Magazine* cover story put it.

The two of us met soon after the article appeared. The more we talked, the more we became determined to get this information out to the world. And from our respective positions, as the leaders of the Harvard Project on Women's Psychology and Girls' Development and the Ms. Foundation for Women, we felt we could, and must, ally to share this information with others.

Marie began to convene the women at the Ms. Foundation to discuss girls' issues. The research on girls struck a chord (or perhaps a nerve)

with the women at the organization. It resonated deeply and pro-
foundly. The more we read and learned, and the more we collaborated
with the Harvard researchers, the more often we said: Yes, that was
me—confident at eleven, confused at sixteen.

With the research in hand—and, in this case, heart—the Ms. Foundation decided to approach this work on girls in a way that we recommend to everyone reading this book. We wrote letters to each other. In
the letters we described our own growing-up experiences—what we
remembered about our preadolescent selves and what happened to us
when our bodies began the surprising, scary, exciting, strange morph
into adolescence. When we read each other's letters, we were moved—
and surprised—by the echoes of similarity.

As diverse as we were, and as able as we all had become, each of us
had walked a familiar path: We all remembered an early time of feeling
brave and free, bold and full of self-pride; we all moved through a voice-
silencing, spirit-stifling transition—as our bodies evolved, as our relationships with our mothers changed, as we developed sexual feelings,
and as the world began to see us in women's bodies.

For the women at the Foundation, these letters became significant.
Reading them, we suddenly became aware of what taking on this work
would mean. Just as the women who began this work at the Harvard
project had found, this work on girls would challenge us in ways that
our other programs and issues had not. In order to lead, we would need
to face down our own adolescent losses. But we also realized that we
could tap into our early girlhood strength.

It became clear that the gains of this struggle would be enormous. In
addition to gains for girls, there would be equally rich gains for women,
all women.

Our hunch was confirmed immediately as some women from the
Ms. Foundation and Elizabeth Debold, a member of the Harvard Project, began to travel the country and talk to groups of women about girls'
development. In city after city, we asked our audiences to undertake the
same exercise we had tried: Think about your preadolescent self and
your transition into adolescence.

What were you like? What happened to you as you grew? What
messages did you hear about being a woman?

Sure enough, the women we met wanted to talk about their experiences. While race, region, class, and culture certainly shaped these experiences, the basic story line of transition—intense strength followed by deep loss—was clear. And so was the response. These meetings across the country told us that we had to take action on this issue. Women strongly wanted to change this experience for their daughters.

Our first thought was to be activists and mothers: to tell people about the research findings as a way to call attention to the problems girls face—their struggle to maintain their sense of self-worth at adolescence, the silencing, the focus on bodies and beauty. But the more we thought, and the more we talked to and observed girls, the more we became interested in young girls' strength. The research was clear: Nine, ten-, and eleven-year-old girls were resilient and confident. While the problems called out for solutions, the issue we kept returning to with fascination was girls' unabashed sureness and sense of self.

Once we acknowledged this, a revolutionary thought began to dominate our discussions: What if this confidence could be tapped—and maintained? What if girls didn't have to lose self-esteem? Our blood quickened.

The women at the Ms. Foundation spent the better part of two years thinking about how we could help caring adults actively intervene in girls' lives. We discussed and discarded several campaigns.

The two of us hatched an idea at one point. We fantasized about a campaign called "A girl is watching; what is she learning?" It would be a consciousness-raising campaign, with public-service announcements and stickers bearing this slogan. We would air the PSAs after commercials and programs on television that portrayed women in a way that both women and girls knew to be unrealistic and inauthentic. Our idea was to let America know that girls were watching all the images we put before them, and they were learning from the subtle and not-so-subtle messages. While a good idea, like many of the others, for now this one remained in the fantasy stage.

But we knew we were on the right track. The goal was to help parents confirm girls' intuition about the realities of their lives, and to help girls mine the sense of self and strength they feel quite naturally. We were sure that if we did this, girls would be able to draw on this reserve of confidence as they hit the rocky road of puberty.

We knew we wanted a public-education campaign and we knew it had to be action-oriented, so we set about compiling information, plans, notes, and ideas. We wanted it to be do-able, so parents and others could act immediately. It also needed to be change-oriented, so girls could see the effects of taking positive, concrete action.

Fortunately, around this time, we met a communications consultant named Nell Merlino. We dumped our two years' worth of thinking into her very creative lap.

In the early '90s, Nell worked with ABC news anchorman Peter Jennings at an AIDS commemorative service; he had chosen to read an essay written by his daughter as part of his remarks. Nell told us the essay contained the very voice of strength and authority we had been talking about and wanted to preserve. Jennings had validated his daughter's voice by, quite literally, "taking her to work" with him.

That's how we came to look at this really basic activity of taking girls to work. The more we looked, the more we felt it might have the right ingredients:

- Adults could be visibly involved with pre- and early-adolescent girls in a positive way.
- Girls could be valued in a place Americans know they would need to be valued—the workplace.
- Girls could have a space and time of their own—to be visible and to be heard.
- We could use the event to call adults' attention to the transition girls go through—and what they could do about it.

The Ms. Foundation decided to stage a trial run in New York. Over the course of a few months, we contacted hundreds of New York City businesses, city agencies, and associations and asked them to let girls join them for a day, the fourth Thursday in April 1993. We created exercises, discussion guides, and sample activities—based on the Harvard Project's research—that adults could try with the girls.

Before the event, Gloria Steinem, one of the Ms. Foundation's founders, was at the office to discuss our plans. After our meeting, Gloria had a meeting with Walter Anderson, the editor of *Parade* magazine. "Janie Appleseed" that she is, Gloria told him what we were planning— and why. The idea struck Walter (a phenomenon we would see over and over), and he ran an item in *Parade*.

That changed everything. Our local experiment became a national event overnight. As a result of the mention in *Parade*, thousands upon thousands of calls poured into our office from across the country. What had struck a chord with us had also resonated around the country. The message in all the calls was the same: "I've seen this change. That's my daughter you're talking about. I've been looking for a way to help. Can we take our daughters to work, too?"

Mothers, fathers, friends, employers, godparents, aunts, and uncles— America wanted to take its daughters to work. And, miracle of miracles, seven women and a fax machine at the Ms. Foundation for Women pulled off the largest public education campaign in the history of the women's movement. In a nutshell, that's how Take Our Daughters to Work day was born.

At this point, we have spent six years working to build a lifetime of confidence for girls. Millions and millions of girls aged nine to fifteen have gone to work each year, and we've alerted this country to the strengths and problems of girls, and of boys as well.

This book, *Girls Seen and Heard*, is our effort to make the lessons we have learned available in an accessible, reader-friendly format. This book has been written in response to need: the deluge of calls, letters, faxes, and e-mails we have received and responded to over the years. Time and again we have been asked: How can we build girls' confidence not just on one day, but every day?

This book attempts to cover that ground. We say "attempts" because there is no surefire answer or guaranteed formula. In fact, the work of helping girls maintain their confidence depends less on what we tell them and more on what we show them—a far more difficult proposition.

This is one of the major lessons we learned from Take Our Daughters to Work day. We might think girls are learning about jobs and careers when they visit us every year in April. But our experience tells us something different. While girls are certainly interested in all that they see and do when they interact with adults on Take Our Daughters to Work day, what they're really studying is us and the quality of our lives.

A few years into this program, the two of us got to see our original campaign fantasy realized. Our initial idea had been on the mark: Girls were watching and girls were learning. In 1995, we made the slogan a theme of the day and a centerpiece of our public-education materials. "A girl is watching. What is she learning?" was emblazoned on our T-shirts and explained to adults in all our literature. We began to alert adults to the fact that girls absorb our very subtle interactions and the messages and ideas we put before them—at work, at home, and in the media.

Recently, we've learned more about this dynamic. In 1997, on the fifth anniversary of Take Our Daughters to Work day, we asked girls to write essays about their experiences. We wanted to hear from girls who first participated in the day at age nine or ten, and who had gone through the transition we had hoped to influence. We wanted to know how their participation had affected them, what they had learned, and how (or if) they had changed.

We received hundreds of stories. Some girls wrote about the jobs they didn't know women could hold—and about jobs they never even knew existed. But the stories were really more about the job holders than the jobs themselves. Girls wrote about how moved they were by the dedication of their parents—not just professional high-powered executives, but mothers and fathers in all different types of jobs. They wrote about the relationships they developed, especially with adults who had talked openly and honestly to them. Girls wrote about the respect and self-pride they felt when adults had treated them with respect, had asked about their dreams (not their dresses), and had viewed them as thinking, learning beings.

A great number of girls wrote about being amazed at how hard their mothers worked during the day—and how often mothers also assumed the major responsibility for work done at night, in the home.

As you read this book, we hope you will keep this in mind. Girls are looking quite intently at our lives—at how we act with them and with one another, at when we speak up and when we choose silence, at how we resolve conflict and deal with power. And—this is crucial—they aren't looking for perfection, for perfect women with perfect jobs. Just as when we were young, being a "perfect girl" is still a strong and often debilitating theme in girls' lives. We should be careful not to reinforce it with myths about our own lives.

Girls are looking for truths and realities, women's truths and realities. There's a story from the first Take Our Daughters to Work day, in 1993, that reflects this idea. A high-level female executive at Brooklyn Union Gas was one of the featured speakers at an assembly held for the girls. When it came time for questions, one of the girls raised her hand and said, "I noticed your job is boring. Did you ever want to do anything else?" The woman, suddenly a bit serious, said that she had always dreamed of being a singer. Unschooled in the art of not asking for what you want, the girl said, "Would you sing me a song?" Sure enough, quietly at first and then belting for all she was worth, the woman started to sing "The Way We Were" to the whole assembly and in front of all her colleagues.

Girls are listening for our songs—the ones we may have forgotten. In fact, it is girls who remind adult women about the parts of ourselves that we have cut off, the songs we have stopped singing. Talking with girls, and listening to them reflect back to us, invites us to bring those parts of ourselves back into the world.

We hope that will happen as you read this book. But it will require a great deal of honesty as you undertake the activities on the following pages. We urge you to read every chapter of this book, asking how the lesson applies to your own life. This will help you when it comes time to talk to your daughter with sincerity, compassion, and even humor about your own feelings and decisions regarding your body, your work, or choosing a life partner.

Of course, the advice of this book needs to be kept in context. We need to be mindful of the climate we live in today. While we seek to be the locus of courage and go-for-it energy, we are also charged with keeping girls safe in a world that can be, and often is, antithetical to their safety. Helping girls to be seen and heard will be compromised unless we work to change our communities so that a girl who is visible and heard is not also hurt.

If you are a mother, aunt, godmother, or grandmother, it can be helpful to find a circle of friends to talk with while you read. When we started this work, we were surprised at how many feelings and emotions about our own girlhoods, once conjured up, clamored to get out. Having your courage and your own stories supported by other women is key. A guide to forming such a circle can be found on page 199.

This book does come with one caution: There may be some lessons we will have to unlearn and some myths we will need to recognize as just that—this business about being perfect is just the start.

One myth says the goal of adolescence is to separate from your daughter. We see it another way. The goal is to build a strong relationship with your daughter, based on her evolving differently. As psychologist Terri Apter's research concludes, adolescent girls want to been seen for who they are and trusted with the truth.

You may also need to unlearn the lesson that being strong means going it alone. One of the secrets to resilience for girls comes when girls work with others to change the conditions that limit all of us, especially women. Your daughter's health depends on her learning to work with others to change a world that tries to stifle women's leadership.

Then there's the you-can-be-anything myth. Any book that tells girls they can be anything they want to be denies the real world that we (and girls and boys) know exists. The role of parenting, taking care of communities and families, is still primarily the strenuous, if rewarding, work of women. No one can be anything they want to be—girl or boy, woman or man—until this unequal division of public and private labor is changed.

Finally, don't buy any line that says to be for your daughter is to be against your son. Only fear speaks in such a voice. To be for girls is also to be for boys. Many men today are seeking to change their own lives by deepening their fathering and their relationships. We need to support men and boys in this. In fact, doing so is the only way to ensure that the lives of our sons and daughters will be full—and full of potential.

As you proceed, you may feel like stifling the songs of your childhood. Please don't. You may not see it at first, but these will be a comforting kind of music for your daughter's ears—the ones that will help her find her own way to dance.

Carol Gilligan, Ph.D.
The Patricia Albjerg Graham Professor of Gender Studies,
Harvard University
Board Member, Ms. Foundation for Women

Marie C. Wilson, M.S.
President, Ms. Foundation for Women

Introduction

During the early 1990s, a full thirty years after Betty Friedan's *The Feminine Mystique* became a clarion call that resulted in the second wave of the women's movement in America, a spate of research revealed some troubling news about our nation's daughters. In spite of three decades of progress toward the goal of women's full and fair participation in this society, the emerging generation of girls showed signs of plummeting self-esteem as young as the age of ten, and certainly by the teen years. Up until adolescence, young girls exhibit a strong and distinct sense of self-confidence, but on the threshold of womanhood, many become insecure about their own judgment and emotions.

Researchers attribute this shift to a constellation of factors, but the primary cause is that at adolescence, girls start to be treated as women. In large measure, this reflects the changes in their bodies. As girls' bodies mature, they are viewed differently by the world, more superficially and sexually. Making matters worse, at the very moment when appearance takes on an inordinate importance for girls, our culture bombards them with unrealistic and dangerous images of women's beauty. Not surprisingly, girls begin not to trust the way they see the world, and as a consequence, the vast majority of girls lower their expectations about the future. The result is that most of them experience depression and feel increased self-doubt. Girls' preoccupation with appearance—and the need for some control over it—causes many girls to develop eating disorders. They also worry about their safety, since they are now the object of uncomfortable sexual attention from boys and men. For some girls, these changes lead to experimentation with sex, and the greatly increased possibility of early pregnancy and sexually transmitted diseases, including HIV. In addition, the rate of attempted suicide for girls is at an alarming all-time high.

The low self-esteem of adolescent girls also has an impact on their performance in school. The focus on appearance—and how boys view them—prevents many girls from competing with boys or excelling in front of boys. In addition, many teachers unintentionally reinforce gender stereotypes by paying more attention to boys in class. This is partly because at the same time girls turn inward, boys deal with their issues at adolescence by acting out—clowning and misbehaving. The sum of this amounts to a disturbing situation for adolescent girls: the strong, optimistic sense of self so evident in girls at age ten or eleven disappears from view.

We now know, however, that this tragic loss doesn't have to occur. Remember, the good news is that our daughters start out strong and healthy, and experience has taught us that a powerful intervention at the onset of distress can curtail or even prevent a change for the worse. If, when girls are at the portal of puberty, we help them feel valued for their talents, personalities, and abilities—and not just for the way they look—there is a strong chance that they won't divest themselves of the buoyant and self-possessed spirits that are the legacy of their childhood. Instead, they will heighten their aspirations, and they will keep the confidence they need in order to reach their full potential.

One key to that end, as we have learned over the years, is to strengthen girls' connection to parents, to mentors—and to each other. Being welcomed into the lives of real women shows girls what their own lives could be like in the future—in spite of the fact that society, from TV and movies to billboards and toys, tells a vastly different story.

In addition, we now know that focusing positive attention on girls' abilities, urging girls to speak their minds, encouraging girls to trust their own judgment, standing with girls when they choose to stand up to the inequities in the world, and stressing how important it is to work hard in school all go a long way toward keeping girls' self-esteem intact. They become what psychologists call "resilient"—that is, able to bounce back in the face of setbacks and go forward with renewed vigor, and to find the courage to change the stresses and conditions that conspire to knock them down again. They also learn what psychologists call "resistance"—the moral courage to be true to themselves instead of subscribing to a culturally dictated norm.

That is why this book was written. We wanted to share with you what we have discovered so that you can put the principles into practice for every girl whose life you touch. Each strategy we suggest for keeping your daughter resilient is based on what we have learned through Take Our Daughters to Work day, as well as years of work with our own Girls, Young Women and Leadership program that funds organizations focusing on the needs and lives of girls. The "hardiness" measures we are using with our grantees—strategies that enhance girls' capacity to resist and transform stress, as well as to increase their knowledge, action, and connection to others—are embedded in every chapter of this book. You will see that *control, commitment, critical consciousness,* and *connection*—qualities that researchers such as Suzanne Ouellette, Ph.D., of the City University of New York, have helped the Ms. Foundation for Women identify—are central to the ideas, activities, and resources we have compiled for you.

We have given you a whole year of life lessons. There is also a unique interactive component running through the book for you to share with your daughter. It is designed to help her take charge of her life and maintain her self-esteem. Also in the book are suggestions for further reading, recommendations of videos to watch together with your daughter, addresses of web sites to visit, and contact information for organizations that can make a difference in your daughter's life—and yours.

That, in fact, is the real beauty of all that we have come to understand. As we help our daughters, we help ourselves as well. Through helping our daughters retain their sense of self-worth, we may regain ours. When our daughters' voices ring out in search of truth and fairness, we are reminded of own need to speak up. As we help our daughters stop hesitating and begin to move with purpose and promise toward womanhood, we may find our own steps becoming sure and swift as well.

Since 1993, the Ms. Foundation for Women has led millions of girls through the doors of industry and to the gateways of possibility. Since 1972, the Foundation has pioneered research to make certain that our daughters' march toward self-esteem is a one-way trip. Now we offer you this manual to help you expand the lessons of a favorite day into the habits of a lifetime for every girl you cherish—and for yourself as well.

Part One

Believe in Yourself

Girls Learn from What They See

ake Our Daughters to Work has a slogan: "A girl is watching. What is she learning?" That slogan came from Dr. Carol Gilligan's germinal research on women's importance to girls' lives. Girls learn what it means to be a woman by watching women. They watch their mothers, their aunts, their grandmothers, their teachers. That is why the key to raising healthy daughters is for adults to do the best they can to lead healthy lives themselves, not only in the physical sense but in the sense of maintaining self-respect and a connection to others.

In their best-selling book *Mother Daughter Revolution*, authors Elizabeth DeBold, Marie C. Wilson, and Idelisse Malavé put it this way: "Girls glean women's reality bit by bit as they watch their mothers maneuver through the daily politics of family life." Girls are moved by daily successes—a mother whose voice counts in family decision making, a father who treats his wife with genuine affection and respect, grandparents who are caring and cared for, workloads that are shared fairly. Girls see when their mothers are happy—and when they're not.

That's why, when your daughter asks about something she has observed, you need to be as honest as you can with her. She wants and deserves answers to her questions. Of course, common sense tells you not to dump all your problems on a nine-year-old, and you're absolutely right. But when a girl picks up on something that makes her wonder what's going on, and then asks a question about the situation, don't silence her, even though her concern may seem trivial to you. For example, one woman who is a TV producer made decisions all day at work, but by evening, she was ready to let others do the deciding. When the family ordered in Chinese food, her husband would say he wanted the chicken with broccoli and her eight-year-old daughter would say she wanted shrimp lo mein, but the mother would say she really didn't care. Finally one evening, the daughter said, "Mommy, why do you always give up on what you want?" The mother was startled by this question and not really sure of the answer. But she didn't cop out. She thought for a while and finally said, "I make decisions all day, and since the three of us always share the dishes we order, I want to pick something you and Daddy might like." Her daughter's quick response was, "But Mommy, I want to know what *you* like!"

Your daughter wants to know what you like, and she also wants to know what you *are* like. Take the time to tell her about things she might not be able to learn from watching you now. Let her know why you chose to make, or not to make, certain decisions. Share stories of how you succeeded or laughed or played or mourned even before she was born. Give her a complete picture of you so that she can begin to comprehend and appreciate the fullness of your being. Let her realize that while your family may be the center of your life, it is not the circumference of your life. That will give her, as she approaches her own womanhood, the joyous realization that she, too, can reach for a satisfying and multifaceted life.

> **W**e think back through our mothers if we are women.
> **Virginia Woolf**

Even more important, however, is to do a little self-examination in an effort to understand what kind of messages you are giving your daughter by the way you behave. The old adage that goes "Actions speak louder than words" is apt here, so make it a point to "watch" yourself. In any given situation, step outside yourself for a moment and figure out what your daughter saw that taught her something—whether positive or negative—about what it means to be a woman. A little girl who watches her father wield power as King of the Remote, who registers the fact that Dad is always in the driver's seat, and who picks up on the fact that Mom never seems to have an opinion about which restaurant to go to is getting broadsided with very discouraging cues about what it means to be a woman. The situation is worse when Mom works as hard as Dad but takes on the whole second shift at home. A daughter who sees two parents sharing all the work outside but not the family responsibilities can only conclude that it's not fair to be a female if you have to put in even more effort than a male does, but you don't even get to pick what you want for dinner.

A lot of women, while ostensibly strong, are actually too nice for their own good. If you find that you fit that description—and so many of us do—resolve to try to make some changes. Are you sacrificing your voice, your very self, in order to be "perfect"? If so, see if you can move a little closer to showing your daughter that you count and tell her where you're still working on making yourself count. That way, when she watches you, she'll learn how to be a person who counts, from the smallest detail of her life to the largest endeavor she'll ever undertake, whatever that may turn out to be as the years go by.

The Ms. Foundation for Women has another slogan: "If all you're ever told is to be a good girl, how do you ever grow up to be a great woman?" Women want their daughters, as well as all the girls whose lives they touch, to grow up to be great women. And girls want to grow up to be great women. We're all working toward the same goal. The key is for women to do the best they can and, beyond that, to let girls know they can go even further, with the assurance that they'll be backed up and supported. You may sometimes decide to be silent rather than to rock the boat, and that's fine as long as you let your daughter know you've made a choice. Also, let her know that in a similar situation, she might choose to be bolder. We instinctively want to protect our daughters, and sometimes—knowing all too well that speaking one's mind can lead to being hurt because our culture encourages silence in our daughters—we teach our daughters to keep the peace rather than to take a risk. We need to teach our daughters that they have two options, and the right to exercise either one, depending on the circumstances. One of those options is to accept the status quo and the other one is to question it. Let your daughter know that the judgment call is hers. That is a very empowering lesson for her to take with her into the future.

Activity 1: I'm a Girl Worth Watching

This is a project that will evolve as you and your daughter proceed through this book. Start by getting the following supplies:

- a loose-leaf notebook
- enough packets of dividers so that you have fifty-two
- lined filler paper
- plain filler paper
- prepunched pocket-style inserts
- crayons, markers, pens, and pencils
- scissors and glue
- an inexpensive camera and film (the disposable kind is fine)

Have your daughter put the title I'M A GIRL WORTH WATCHING on the cover of the notebook, along with her byline. Then she can decorate the cover to reflect who she is. She might want to make a collage of images and phrases cut out of magazines, or she can use snapshots of herself from babyhood on, leaving room for some exciting new ones she might add during the course of creating her book.

The pocket inserts are for collecting newspaper items, pictures, and advertisements from magazines; memorabilia from her life during the time she's working on this project; snapshots; random thoughts she jots down to use later; and so on. Remember, her book is not a scrapbook in the traditional sense. It is a reflection of who she is and who she is becoming in the context of the world around her.

For her first entry, have her put the title PEOPLE I WATCH on the divider flap and on the first page. Now ask her to make two columns. The column on the left is for a list of people—men and women—whom she admires. She should stick to contemporary people; since a later activity will deal with historical figures. The column on the right is for enumerating what she admires about each person—traits, accomplishments, life choices. Let her know that this whole project will always be in flux and that she will be free to go back and change, delete, or add to the entries she makes as she learns more about herself and her world.

Also, take an interest in what she writes and encourage her to talk about why she has made her choices and her comments. Get her to examine them. If she lists Fiona Apple in the left column and writes "because she's skinny" in the right column, she has given you a wonderful opportunity to question the cultural stereotype about women's looks, and to explore the importance of a woman's talents and abilities and strength of character. And if she has trouble coming up with heroines of substance, help her out. Again, there is no rush and you don't have to "finish" this section.

Activity 2: For My Eyes Only

The preceding project is a public one, a way for your daughter to proclaim her burgeoning sense of self-worth for everyone to see and hear about. This project, on the other hand, is a private one. All your daughter needs is a diary or blank book. What she's going to write will be more than diary entries, however. You want her to use the technique of journaling. Encourage her to delve into her feelings and reactions, and also to write about hopes and dreams, instead of simply writing down the events of the day ("Me and Jenny went to a Hanson concert"). What did she see and hear today that taught her something or made her wonder about something or changed her opinion or made her mad or gave her the courage of her convictions? Journaling is a very powerful tool for getting in touch with one's self. (Why not do some journaling of your own so that you, too, can keep growing? Many women report that they are amazed at how this seemingly simple activity has changed their lives.)

Resources

Mother Daughter Revolution: From Good Girls to Great Women, by Elizabeth DeBold, Marie Wilson, and Idelisse Malavé (New York: Bantam

Books, 1994). This book and its complementary discussion guide have suggestions for forming a mother-daughter group, topics to explore, and activities for both generations.

Where She Came From: A Daughter's Search for Her Mother's History, by Helen Epstein (Boston: Little, Brown, 1997).

2

Girls Should Be Seen and Heard

Developmental psychology has shown that boys and girls have a different timetable for maturation and different tasks to deal with during the growing process. One result of this asynchrony is that while boys have special challenges during early childhood, most girls do very well up until about the age of ten, as we noted earlier. At that point, however, a dramatic shift occurs. Boys typically come into their own just as girls hit what Gilligan calls "the wall of adolescence." The immediate problem for girls at adolescence remains the fact that while their bodies are ever more noticeable, they begin to fall into the shadows. That is precisely why girls need to be encouraged to be seen and heard—and that realization, as we have mentioned previously, was the impetus for Take Our Daughters to Work day.

Now it's time for you to put the principles of the public education campaign to work for you in your daughter's daily life. You can start right at home by paying attention to the dynamics of your family and learning to pick up on situations in which your daughter isn't getting her turn.

For example, here's what went on one evening in one household:

Moira, who had recently turned twelve, was poking at the peas on her plate and fidgeting in her chair. Her brother Scott, two years older than she, was holding court at the family dinner table, going on and on about how he won the Math Olympiad and how he made the travel team for soccer. The only other person in this blended family getting any attention was six-year-old David, who, when he wasn't bleating "Scuse me! Scuse me!" was occupying himself by kicking Jessica under the table. Jessica was eleven and not amused. Except for "Stop it!" she didn't say a word during the entire meal.

Sound familiar? Scenes similar to this one go on at dinner tables nightly all across the country. Simply put, most parents, however well meaning, don't realize that their daughters aren't getting anything like equal time stage center. Also, you don't need an expert to tell you that girls on the threshold of adolescence typically morph from feisty and forthcoming kids into silent if not downright sullen beings who no longer fight for attention but shrink from it. Here's some proof anyway: A report commissioned jointly by *Seventeen* magazine and the Ms. Foundation for Women showed that adolescent girls lose self-confidence, are not comfortable standing up for themselves, have trouble handling criticism, and are likely to be overwhelmed by other people's emotional needs when making decisions or taking action.

Given all this, is there anything you can do to make sure your daughter's voice rings out and gets ratified? Definitely. Right at home, you can make a concerted effort to draw your daughter out and let her know that what's on her mind matters a lot. By creating an environment in which girls can be heard, you'll also be sending the message that their triumphs and failures and fears are important. Think about how a talk show host works. If she has two or more guests, she makes certain that nobody dominates the conversation. Every now and then, she'll say something such as, "How fascinating, John. What do *you* think about that, Jane?" She turns and makes eye contact with Jane and smiles expectantly. That's how she keeps the conversational ball bouncing from one person to another without appearing to interrupt anybody. Notice that she also asks "essay questions" that elicit stories and opinions.

You don't have to be Oprah to use those techniques at home. You can wait until somebody draws a breath and then say something like "That is really neat, Carlos! I'm glad you got along better with Mr. Smith in the resource room this afternoon. How about you, Isabelle? How was band practice today?" In other words, even if you do rein Carlos in a bit, if all you say to Isabelle is "How was your day?" you're not likely to get her to open up. But if you give her something specific to start with, she'll have a way to get going. Then, with a little encouragement, she'll probably go on to other topics as well.

Of course, this strategy involves remembering which day she has band practice, her friends' names, and plenty of other details about your daughter's life as well. Your daughter will feel much better about herself and her life if you show her that you've been paying attention to what she says, and that you care about her enough to remember the things she tells you that are important to *her*. That way, the next time she opens up to you, she won't have to start from ground zero. Be the sounding board she needs in order to hear her thoughts resonate and find a measure of their worth, effectiveness, and acceptability.

There may be areas of your daughter's life, however, that are hard for you to hear about and difficult for you to talk about. Why not grab a friend and explore with her what those uncomfortable topics bring up about your own girlhood? Discovering and acknowledging where you have difficulty and where you have silenced voices, including your own, will help you listen to your daughter—and may even heal what hurts you.

But what about school? Is there any way you can ensure that your daughter gets the chance she needs to speak up and be counted? Your best bet is to be as involved a parent as you possibly can. If possible, save some vacation days so you can help out during the science fair or go on a field trip. While you're with the class, make a mental note of whether or not the teacher unwittingly allows boys to dominate and to relegate girls to stereotypical "helpmate" roles. Also, look around the classroom and the halls to see whether the bulletin boards reflect the fact that women constitute over half of the world's population. Look through the textbooks for the same reason. If you find inequities, make an appointment to speak with the teacher, the principal, or even the superintendent. These problems are ones that most teachers and schools want to correct. Show them you're an ally. Suggest some changes and resources such as the ones following each chapter of this book. By helping to ensure that all girls are seen and heard, you'll be instrumental in preparing them for succeeding in the world they'll inherit in the millennium to come.

Activity: I Am Seen and Heard

This is divider flap 2 in your daughter's I'M A GIRL WORTH WATCHING notebook. She can draw pictures or paste in snapshots of herself, and write about her personal moments of stepping forward and speaking up. Maybe she voiced an opinion during a family discussion, or maybe she's involved in a student theater group that presents skits for younger students about saving the environment. Maybe she plays the cello and was in a concert. Maybe she has a great sense of humor and her friends count on her to help them look on the light side. As always, her entries are not carved in stone, and as she and the project both grow, she can add new filler pages, make notes about how her values and opinions are changing, and revise anything she once put in.

Resource

Growing a Girl: Seven Strategies for Raising a Strong, Spirited Daughter, by Dr. Barbara Mackoff (New York: Dell, 1996).

3

Know Thyself

The message on the Delphic Oracle in Greece, inscribed circa 600 B.C., is "Know Thyself." Some things never change. As of this writing, people—and girls in particular—are still sorely in need of that pithy but profound piece of advice. Your daughter needs your help in order to understand why this is vital to her health and happiness. And again, as an adult fostering a girl's quest for self-knowledge, you will learn more about yourself as well. You may even reactivate dreams long deferred and resolve to pursue them after all. As George Eliot wrote, "It is never too late to be who you might have been."

Work with your daughter to create the following three lists. You can work on all three simultaneously, jotting down ideas on one or the other as they occur to you. These future-focused activities are based on the research of life/work specialists who have shown that the skills we most enjoy remain fairly constant throughout our lives. Helping your daughter identify and begin to apply those skills in her work and her hobbies will go a long way toward making sure that her life's energy will be spent in ways that will allow her not simply to survive, but to thrive:

1) *Things she likes to do.* Tell your daughter not to censor this list in any way. Even if she thinks something is trivial or time-wasting or controversial or nontraditional, she should put it down anyway. The one and only criterion is that the activity must be something she truly enjoys. For example, Michelle, a thirteen-year-old, came up with the following: "playing with my cat, figuring out how to save and spend the money I make doing yard work, watching the Discovery Channel, playing softball, e-mailing my friends."

2) *Things she thinks she would enjoy doing.* Remind your daughter that in thinking up this list, she might be inspired by books she's read, shows she's watched on TV, work sites she's visited, experiences other people have told her about, and virtual places she's been to on the Internet. Michelle wrote the following: "rock climbing, visiting ancient history places in Greece and Egypt, working in a laboratory like the one I visited last year, teaching kids in countries that don't have good education systems, track, horseback riding."

3) *Things she doesn't like to do.* Michelle's included "sitting still for a long time, practicing the piano (but I do it anyway)."

Clearly, Michelle is a girl with wide-ranging interests and tremendous potential. If you were her parent or mentor and you sat down with her and her lists, the idea would be to talk about all of the pursuits her interests might lead to. For example, playing with the cat might point to a career as a veterinarian, zookeeper, or biologist; keeping track of her yard-work earnings might mean an interest in high finance, although probably not a career as an accountant, given her stated aversion to sitting still. Also, there's certainly an adventurer in there somewhere. She yearns to get out and try new things. Maybe she could be an anthropologist? A foreign correspondent? An Outward Bound instructor? And then there are Michelle's nascent computer skills and her interest in science to consider. Finally, Michelle deserves a pat on the back for sticking to her piano studies, even though that's not her favorite activity. She should know that and be reminded that, while there may not be a career as a pianist on the horizon for her, disciplining herself to practice those scales will translate into good work habits no matter what she ends up doing. Not only that, but recent research has shown that girls who study music do better in math!

How exciting to explore what a girl with her whole future ahead of her could do, and how wonderful to let her know that enjoying what she does is not only a possibility, *but the very first requirement of whatever becomes her calling.* Her life's work, after all, should not be drudgery. It should, in the end, be as meaningful as it is gainful. Help her make that happen. (And don't forget to dust off your own dreams while you're at it!)

> **M**y world did not get smaller because I was a black female writer. It just got bigger.
>
> Toni Morrison, Nobel Prize–winning author

Activity: This Is Who I Am

The third chapter in I'M A GIRL WORTH WATCHING can include the lists your daughter made about her interests and the career choices they point to. Then, whenever she finds a new interest—maybe she gets to go horseback riding on a school trip or takes up a new sport—she can add to her lists.

Resource

Let's Talk About Me: A Girl's Personal, Private, and Portable Instruction Book for Life, from Inc Girl Games (New York: Archway, 1997).

Also, a CD-ROM: *Let's Talk About Me: The Girl's Interactive Handbook for the 21st Century* (New York: Simon & Schuster Interactive, 1996).

4

You're the Star of the Show

Many a little girl, inspired by intrepid literary heroines—Jo in *Little Women*, who goes off to New York to become a writer, or Heidi, who saves Klara's life—envisions herself as a potential heroine as well. But then, as childhood wanes and adolescence looms, that powerful sense of being the plucky protagonist in the story of her life begins to slip away. She loses heart. Messages from the media, plus a new kind of attention from boys and men as she develops a woman's body, conspire to make her feel she's not destined to be the smart and spirited central figure in a challenging real-life adventure after all. She finds herself judged for her looks rather than for her brains or abilities. Even a girl who is considered pretty isn't spared. In fact, she is often not taken seriously, as though intelligence and beauty were somehow mutually exclusive.

The solution is to keep reinforcing the fact that your daughter is indeed still the star of her own life, and a worthy and wonderful star at that. In practice, that means continuing to take an interest in her activities and her achievements and making certain she has featured moments just as she did when she was small. For example, maybe you made a big fuss over her birthday up until she was about ten or eleven, giving elaborate parties and letting her wear the birthday girl crown while she sat in the chair of honor and opened her gifts with her guests at her feet. Then, if you're like many parents, as she began to pull away from you in adolescence and look and act too grown-up for such pleasures, you stopped doing that. Suddenly the family album had no more pictures of her as the center of attention, and she celebrated her birthday with her pals at Friendly's and the bowling alley. That's what she seemed to prefer anyway.

The only safe ship in a storm is leadership.

Faye Wattleton

Maybe so, but don't let her fool you. Scratch that adolescent attitude and you'll still find your daughter underneath, as much (if not more) in need as she ever was of being reassured in word and deed that she's one of a kind and dear to your heart. So let her go bowling if she wants to, but surprise her with a family celebration as well. Or plan to do something alone with her as a birthday treat or even for no reason at all—going on an outdoor adventure or going to the air and space museum. There's nothing like having your undivided attention away from siblings to show your daughter that you take her life and her ideas seriously. That will go a long way toward shoring up her self-confidence and getting her to share her thoughts about her life.

And what about school functions and extracurricular activities? Teachers and group leaders alike report that while events for little children typically attract not only parents but grandparents, attendance falls off drastically when students hit their teens. Do you have pictures of every school play from the time she was four until she was ten—and nothing after that? You're not alone. In a similar vein, did you festoon the refrigerator with her finger paintings when she was little but fail to show an interest in her later efforts, let alone display them? Then you're like a lot of parents. Somehow, the signals girls give while they're moving from childhood to womanhood put us off. But we have to persevere. That little girl who used to rush in all excited with a project from school or a note about an upcoming performance made it easy for you to respond to her. The teenager who may now sequester herself in her room and not volunteer any information about her life is harder to reach. But you can do it.

One mother reports that in a moment of nostalgia, she bought her fourteen-year-old daughter a birthday card meant for a little girl. The card featured a cartoon-style bear and came with a button that read "Excellent Daughter." After she got home, this mother had misgivings. Kishauna, her daughter, had seemed so standoffish of late and would probably think the gesture was babyish. But finally, the mother gave her daughter the card. Kishauna did smile, but she didn't say much, and the mother shrugged, thinking she should have trusted her second thoughts and bought a more sophisticated card.

Then the next morning, Kishauna came down to breakfast. The button was pinned to her backpack for all the world to see. And as Kishauna walked out the door to catch the school bus, she gave her mother a hug and handed her a handmade card. The paper was bordered with a design made of x's and o's and the large message in the middle had only two words: "Excellent Mother."

Activity: The Jane Doe Show

This will be the fourth chapter in your daughter's book. Have her substitute her name, and then create a concept for a talk show of which she would be the star. What time of day would it be broadcast? Would it be on radio or TV? Who would be her guests be? What issues would they discuss? What kind of advertising would she accept? Also, your daughter could get together with her friends, boys as well as girls, and do a show live. She can either be serious, or she can create a parody if she's an older teen with a sophisticated sense of humor. Encourage her to poke fun at aspects of the culture that perpetuate gender stereotypes and therefore keep both boys and girls boxed in. Be sure she includes ads in her show.

Resource

All That She Can Be: Helping Your Daughter Maintain Her Self-Esteem, by Dr. Carol Eagle and Carol Colman (New York: Simon & Schuster, 1993).

5

Be Your Own Person

Psychologist Terri Apter, the author of *Altered Loves: Mothers and Daughters During Adolescence*, studied sixty-five mother-daughter pairs in the United Kingdom and the United States to learn how girls separate during adolescence, a task long held to be the central one of the teen years. To her surprise, Apter found that unlike boys—who had been the model for studies up until her work began—girls do not struggle to *sever* relationships but to *redefine* them. They want to become not so much separate from us as they want to become autonomous. There's a big difference. Autonomous individuals can take care of themselves, but they remain emotionally connected to the adults in their lives.

That's very good news. However, achieving autonomy is rarely an easy task for a girl. Listen to Laura, now fifteen: "My mom is the principal of the high school. This is a pretty small town and almost everybody knows her. I have always been really proud to be her daughter, and she has always treated me almost like an equal, talking to me about stuff about her work and everything. It was so cool! I wanted to grow up to be just like her. My dad is cool, too, but he travels a lot for his job so there would be weeks at a time when it was just my mom and me.

"But then I started high school, and I was also dealing with being 'Mrs. Jefferson's daughter.' I felt like I had to live up to that, which was pretty scary, but I also started to resent not being just Laura, just me. And then I would think, Who am I anyway? And I would draw a blank."

Like Laura, most young girls identify closely with their mothers and as a result, they go through a period of self-doubt when they urgently need to discover an individuality of their own. As Apter discovered, separation is not the goal for girls, but instead it's the need to be trusted and seen for who they are. In Laura's case, her mother was wise enough to sense the strain Laura was under and do something about it. For one thing, she encouraged Laura to develop a closer relationship with her godmother, a public defender. And she also suggested that Laura might like to get involved in some volunteer work that had nothing to do with the high school where she was in her mother's shadow.

These two strategies—letting a girl get close to a mentor or "othermother" and letting her shine in a setting that's hers alone—are ideal when a girl is trying to be somebody other than her mother's daughter and yet not lose the connection with her mother altogether. For Laura, one result was that she visited her godmother's office and even went to court with her, and then came home with tales of her experiences. "It was awesome!" she reports. "I had stuff to tell that my mom had never heard about. I was like this expert and she was taking it all in. That made me feel really good."

Beyond that, Laura became a candy striper at the local hospital, and she turned out to have a talent for relating to older patients. One day when her own great-aunt was in for gall bladder surgery, Laura's mother came to visit during Laura's shift. The two of them were walking down the hall and a white-haired woman shuffling along with a cane smiled and said, "You must be Laura's mother!"

"That was like the greatest moment of my life," Laura says. "I wasn't 'Mrs. Jefferson's daughter.' *She* was 'Laura's mother'!"

Activity: The One and Only Jane Doe!

This chapter of the book that your daughter is creating is a little more lighthearted than some. The idea is for her to collect all kinds of evidence that shows what's unique about her. She can draw a self-portrait, and she can write a poem about herself. She can also paste in anything that she thinks typifies her—a piece of sheet music because she plays the piano or a citation she got for winning the speech contest run by the Rotary Club. She can also list her favorite color, song, musician, food, season, sport, teacher. Finally, she can capture some affectionate moments with you when she was being her own person and you were proud of her: a snapshot of the two of you beaming on the day she won the election for student council president; a note you wrote to her on the occasion of her menarche, congratulating her on coming of age; a matchbook from the restaurant where you celebrated her softball team's victory. As always this activity is meant to be open-ended. She can add to her collection anytime she thinks of something that says she's one of a kind.

Resources

Girls Know Best: Written by Girls Just Like You, compiled by Michelle Roehm (Hillsboro, OR: Beyond Words Publishing, 1977).

6

You're the Boss

Girls who get to exercise authority within safe and reasonable boundaries are far less likely to resort to self-destructive ways of defying the status quo. That's why, when it comes to setting limits and letting your daughter know what's expected of her, you are wise if you choose your battles. Obviously, you have to establish some absolutes—be in by 11:00 P.M., finish your homework before you watch TV, wear your helmet when you ride your bike, never get in a car with a drunk driver, write thank-you notes to your grandmother—but wherever possible, foster your daughter's emerging sense of self by allowing her to have some control over her life. If she's lucky enough to have her own room, let her decorate it pretty much any way she wants and resist the urge to tidy it up while she's not around. Certainly, she needs to know that being a slob is not acceptable—not in your house and not in the world she's going to encounter as a grown-up—and leaving plates of food under the bed until mold starts to grow simply won't do. But if she wants to paint each wall a different color and glue a collage on the ceiling over her bed so she can look at it before she falls asleep, so be it.

In the same way, what's the difference if she dyes her hair with green

Kool-Aid as long as she also remembers to floss and brush? Think back to your own youth. Wasn't there something you did, some statement you made, that gave you a rush of power and the feeling that you were in charge of yourself? One mother recalls going to the mall with her best friend and getting her ears pierced. "We were thirteen, and we had saved up our allowances to buy the earrings. I thought I was going to faint, but it barely hurt at all and it was unbelievably exciting. We felt so daring, so grown-up, and kind of wicked, too! Those little gold studs were like talismans, magic charms that warded off evil and gave us superhuman strength." This woman reports that her parents were suitably shocked—that reaction was part of the fun—but that they didn't insist that she take the earrings out. "I thought about that when my own daughter wanted get her head shaved like Sinéad O'Connor," she said. "Her hair was down to her waist, absolutely gorgeous, but I thought, Hey, this isn't the end of the world. At least she's not doing drugs or starving herself."

That's a good point. Girls who feel they have no freedom to make choices in their lives often gain a sense of control over themselves by developing dangerous behaviors. Eating disorders and self-mutilation—cutting and burning one's own body—are on the rise in today's adolescent population, particularly among females. So are suicide attempts. As one young woman who suffered from anorexia in her teens put it, "After a lifetime of trying to please other people and live up to their standards, I had finally found an area where I was in charge." This is a frighteningly typical attitude, according to *Body Politic: Transforming Adolescent Girls' Health*, a report of the proceedings of the 1994 Healthy Girls/Healthy Women Roundtable sponsored by the Ms. Foundation for Women. The report reveals that only 2% of boys but 18% of girls in high school are at serious risk for eating disorders and states, "The eating disorders of anorexia nervosa and bulimia nervosa are closely linked with girls' need to meet the 'perfect girl' or 'good girl' standards, as well as the cultural ideal of the 'superwoman' who is strong and independent, yet feminine and nurturing."

So that your daughter doesn't feel the need to go to such perilous

My ability to survive personal crises is really a mark of the character of my people. Individually and collectively, we react with a tenacity that allows us again and again to bounce back from adversity.

Chief Wilma Mankiller

lengths to feel she's her own boss, give her plenty of opportunities to make choices. If she wants to be a vegetarian, either because she's into animal rights or because she's read that it's healthy, don't object. Support her by doing a little research in order to learn about combining foods to get the right amount of amino acids. And if she wants to wear black nail polish or not shave under her arms or listen to rock music, why argue? Even if she wants a nose ring, that's not so terrible as long as she agrees to take it out when she interviews the mayor for a school project.

And above all, respect her privacy. According to the Center for Adolescent Studies at Indiana University, middle adolescence is prime time for journal keeping, and it goes without saying that you should never read what she writes in her diary. Similarly, don't open her mail, don't purposely eavesdrop on her phone conversations, and don't go through her things. If you're worried that she's prematurely sexually active, confronting her with the condoms you found hidden under her notebook in her desk drawer is certainly not the way to draw her into your confidence. And if you think she's hanging out with the wrong crowd, listening in on what she says to her friends and then bawling her out is only going to drive her away. Instead, treat her with dignity and let her have her own space, literally and figuratively. On the other hand, girls sometimes don't cover their tracks precisely because they *want* you to help them. Stay alert to signals and signs she's giving you. Then make sure you're available for her and that you're someone she can really talk to, because you're someone who will really listen.

Activity: I'm in Charge Here

Have your daughter draw a circle on a blank piece of filler paper. Inside the circle, she can either paste a picture of herself or draw her face, a smiley face, a peace symbol, a tree—anything *she* chooses to have represent herself. Then she should draw lines that look like spokes coming out of the circle. At the end of each spoke, she can draw or write or paste something that she's in charge of—how she wears her hair, what her room looks like, what kind of clothes she wears, what kind of music she listens to, what TV shows are her favorites, what she writes in her journal, what she talks about with her best friend, what she writes to her pen pal, how she spends her money, what she gives people for presents, what she orders in a restaurant, and whatever else she comes up with.

Resources

Eating Disorders Awareness and Prevention, 603 Stewart St., Suite 803, Seattle, WA 98101; 206-382-3587; (web site) http://members@ aol.com/edapinc.

American Anorexia/Bulimia Association, 165 West 46th St., Suite 1108, New York, NY 10036; (212) 575-6200; (web site) http://members @aol.com/amaubu.

7

Stay in Touch with Your Inner Girl

ew experiences in life compare to the surge of power an artist feels
F when she makes something out of nothing. That, after all, is what
creativity amounts to. A painter stares at a blank canvas, a sculptor
starts with a block of marble or a lump of clay, a choreographer hears a
piece of music and sees movement in her mind's eye, a composer sits at
the keyboard and captures the melody she hears in her head, a writer
faces an empty computer screen and conjures up the right words. Eventually, a landscape emerges, or a statue, a dance, a tune, a story—a
brand-new something where once there was nothing.

Fine artists, however, are far from the only people who are creative.
Abraham Maslow, in the second edition of *Toward a Psychology of Being,*
investigates the nature of creativity in what he calls "self-actualizing
people"—those who are emotionally healthy, highly evolved, and
mature. He contends that these fully developed people are creative in
any endeavor, be it organizing a business, bringing up a child, spending leisure time, or nurturing a friendship. "A fair proportion of my subjects, though healthy and creative in the special sense I am going to
describe . . . did not have great talent or genius, nor were they poets,

composers, inventors, artists or creative intellectuals," he wrote. "All my subjects were relatively more spontaneous and expressive than average people. They were more 'natural' and less controlled and inhibited in their behavior, which seemed to flow out more easily and freely with less blocking and self-criticism."

Maslow goes on to say, "Self-actualizing creativeness was in many ways like the creativeness of *all* happy and secure children. . . . Almost any child can compose a song or a poem or a dance or a painting or a play or a game on the spur of the moment. . . . Let us say that [my subjects] had either retained or regained at least two main aspects of child-likeness, namely, they were . . . 'open to experience' and they were spontaneous and expressive. . . . We are dealing with a fundamental characteristic, inherent in human nature, a potentiality given to all or most human beings at birth, which most often is lost or buried or inhibited as the person gets enculturated."

What a tragic thought! In order to help your daughter (and yourself) "retain or regain" that glorious, self-approving sense of spontaneity, try the following:

1) For older girls, here is the first line of a poem by Annie Rogers: "I'm going back for her the way I remember her." You and your daughter can each write two poems or essays beginning with or based on that line. One of your daughter's writings will be about her recollections of herself as a child, and the other will be about how she imagines you were as a child. One of your writings will be about yourself as a child and the other will be your memories of your daughter as a child. Now share your writings by reading them aloud to each other. Talk about what is the same and what is different in your perceptions of yourselves and each other.

2) Look for some passages or verses in what you've written that describe ways of being that got left behind, and then plan a way to recapture those childlike characteristics and actions. One mother wrote:

The years went too quickly, as all mothers mourn.
Wasn't it yesterday that you were born?

When did the time pass since I watched you swing,
A three-year-old charmer, a bird on the wing?
Where has the six-year-old's gap-toothed smile gone?
Where is that cartwheeling kid on the lawn?

As a result, she and her daughter, thirteen at the time, went to the park one fine day. They pushed each other on the swings and did cartwheels and rolled in the grass and laughed until their sides hurt. That night, when the daughter had gotten into her pajamas and brushed her teeth, she padded into the study where her mother, a high-school teacher, was grading papers. The two of them had been at odds for a while there, just somehow disagreeing about every little thing, and there had been many a night when the daughter had flounced upstairs to bed without so much as a "Good night," let alone a kiss. But on this night, she stood in the doorway of the study until her mother realized she was there. Then the girl ran over to her mother and gave her an enormous bear hug, planted a kiss on her cheek, and said with an ear-to-ear smile, "You are like the totally coolest mother on earth. G'night!"

See whether reaching back for the girl she was and the girl you were doesn't work the same magic for you and your daughter.

3) Improvise an Isadora Duncan–style dance with your daughter. Remind each other that because this is your own dance, everything you do is right. You won't judge each other. There's no standard and there are no rules, so there's no such thing as a mistake or a misstep. Beethoven's "Für Elise" or any of the Brahms waltzes are perfect musical accompaniments for this exercise. You can also dance to livelier, more contemporary music, but there's something about these flowing selections that releases the spirit and makes you move in a natural, organic way. You can also put on long, loose skirts if you have them, and use floaty scarves to help you sway, or blow soap bubbles to chase and reach for. You can do this anywhere you have room, but be sure to try it outside on a summer evening at twilight, with the grass between your toes and the wind playing in your hair.

A *Ladies' Home Journal* "Make Your Dreams Come True" contest revealed that the largest number of the respondents, women at midlife, wanted a chance to live in a creative way instead of spending a lifetime "wearing the path between work and home away," as the poet W. H. Auden put it. The common theme was the need to sing anew the song of the spirit. For those midlife women, that song had long since been silenced by a disapproving society.

Don't let that happen to your daughter. And if it has already happened to you, promise yourself to get in touch with your spirit of creativity once again and never let it go.

Activity: The Way We Were

The poems and essays you and your daughter wrote about your girlhood go in this chapter of her book, as well as anything she wants to write and illustrate about the activities you did together to reach back for the girls you once were.

Resource

Singing at the Top of Our Lungs: Women, Love and Creativity, by Jo-Ann Krestan and Claudia Bepko (New York: HarperCollins, 1993).

8

You're Just Right

Ours is a society bent on fixing what's wrong with children at the expense of applauding what's right about them. Yes, finding ways to help students compensate for learning disabilities is important, just as offering speech therapy to a child with a lisp is prudent. But too often in our zeal to correct a perceived problem, we—parents and educators alike—miss the miracle of what makes any given youngster unique. Add to this the fact that girls at puberty are particularly harsh on themselves anyway and the situation becomes serious. Deepak Chopra, M.D., best-selling author and an acknowledged master at melding Eastern and Western philosophies, reminds us that we would do well to keep in mind the East Indian concept of the "dharma." He says that everyone, without exception, has a dharma, or a purpose in life. This means that there is no one else, not even an identical twin, who has your daughter's unique combination of gifts. She may have limitations, but they are not as important as her strengths.

Dr. Chopra regrets the fact that Americans focus so intently on what is not perfect about their children instead of championing what is good about them. Jillian's story is a case in point. Now eighteen and a first-year student at the Fashion Institute of Technology in New York City, she grimaces at the memory of her junior-high-school years. "Tutors, tutors, tutors!" she says. "My family is fortunate enough to be able to afford extra help for me, and it's not that I'm not grateful. I'm dyslexic and they would have done anything for me. But the thing was, in order to fit in special help during school, they had me excused from art, and I had to quit the swim team because it conflicted with my private tutor after school. But art and swimming were my favorite things!"

With good reason: Jillian is a talented artist and a natural athlete. Even though she was denied her art classes in school, she used to spend hours watching a television show about how to make "instant" oil paintings. "I baby-sat every Friday night for the same family and I spent that money on art supplies," she said. "OK, the techniques I learned from the TV were just basic, but I kind of went on from there out of instinct." She points with pride to a framed seascape of hers on the wall, an intriguing swirl of blues and greens illuminated with flecks of gold. "Pretty neat, huh?" she says. Indeed.

As for dropping out of swimming, Jillian coped during seventh and eighth grade by overeating. "I was the total couch potato," she says. Needless to say, this development didn't do much for her self-esteem. Then the summer after she turned thirteen, she went to sleep-away camp for the first time. "It was heaven on earth!" she says. "No tutors, no spelling tests, just fresh air and campfires and swimming and tennis. And arts and crafts. I was the star of the jewelry-making class. We drew designs and made stuff out of metal. Mine won the prize at the showing we had for parents' day. Plus, my swim team won the meet that weekend. It doesn't get much better than that!"

Actually, it did get even better than that for Jillian. She came home feeling spunky and full of herself. Her parents, touched by the exuberance their daughter had displayed when she was in her element, cut down on the tutoring and offered her art classes. Not only that, but she kept up with her tennis and joined the high-school swim team, which she led to victory for three years in a row. She also collected an impressive portfolio and eventually got into FIT, where she is majoring in jewelry design.

"I still can't spell," she says, laughing. "Even the spell checker on my computer can't understand me. Like, I wrote 'cud' for 'could' and the computer didn't correct it because 'cud' is a real word, like what cows chew. Is that a hoot or what?" But Jillian manages by taking a tape recorder to class and she is so comfortable with her disability now that she marches up to any new professor and explains her academic history. "I just get that out of the way right up front," she says. "Then we can get on with the good stuff about me."

And there's plenty of that, certainly, just as there is in every girl. The challenge is to help a girl who is in the throes of self-doubt to stop bemoaning her inadequacies and start celebrating her strengths. Be her cheerleader. Remind her at every turn how amazing she is and how proud you are of her. And as we've mentioned before, you'll be doing yourself a favor if you apply this lesson to yourself as well. Why not sit down with your daughter and write a list of five things that are right about each of you? Anything counts, from having an infectious laugh to being good with children to being a math whiz. Now forget about judging yourselves by some unrealistic standard. You're not too tall or too short or too stupid or too clutzy. You're just right.

Activity: There's No One Else I'd Rather Be Than Me!

Your daughter's list of what's right about herself goes in here. And now that she has loosened up, she may think of many more than five things. She can list as many as she wants and come back to this exercise as often as something occurs to her. She can also illustrate her points.

Resource:

I Am Beautiful: A Celebration of Women in Their Own Words, edited by Dana Carpenter and Woody Winfree (Berkley: Rose Communications, 1997).

9

Get a Life You Love

Sometimes even when we mean well, we keep our daughters from finding their own way in life. We try to guide them because we love them so very much and we want them to be happy and secure. However, our good intentions can sometimes end up stifling our daughters' growth—and with it, their self-esteem.

That is what almost happened to a girl named Tamika. Tamika's mother wanted her to be a schoolteacher. Over and over again, she would tell Tamika that teachers can get jobs anywhere, even if their husbands are transferred. She would say that teaching is something you can fall back on. She would say that while teachers don't make as much as, say, brain surgeons, they make a darn good living, especially if they have a master's degree. She would point out that teachers have a strong union and a good retirement plan. And she would underscore the fact that teachers have the same schedule as their kids so they can be home to do the milk-and-cookie thing and have summers off. All of this, Tamika's mother would say, makes teaching an ideal profession for a woman. She herself had never gone to college, so she had been stuck her whole life in low-paying jobs with long hours, and if she had it to do over, she'd find a way to get her teaching certificate somehow. But since that was all water under the bridge, she figured she'd give Tamika the opportunity she never had.

There was only one problem. Tamika didn't want to be a schoolteacher. She had nothing against teaching and in fact thought it was a noble profession, but she didn't enjoy dealing with children and she didn't like being cooped up inside. The thought of a lifetime spent in a classroom full of kids gave her the shivers. However, up until Tamika was fourteen, she had no clear idea of exactly what she *did* want to do, so she never bucked her mother. She would just nod numbly when she got the schoolteacher speech for the umpteenth time.

Then something wonderful happened. A new family moved into the apartment building where Tamika lived in New York City. Tamika made friends with the kids, a twelve-year-old girl and a ten-year-old boy. She found out that their mother was something called an Urban Ranger. The mother had a green uniform and she strapped a cool pack around her waist with binoculars and water bottles and bug spray in it, and she led groups of people on hikes and bird-watching trips through the Green Belt on Staten Island, a forest and nature preserve. She had a degree in botany, and she could identify any plant she saw.

The first duty of a human being is to assume the right relationship to society—more briefly, to find your real job and do it.

Charlotte Perkins Gilman

She had also minored in biology, and she knew a lot about animals. Once, Tamika got to go on an all-day hike with her. She saw a blue heron in a pond dotted with frogs on lily pads. She saw persimmon trees with bark like perfectly placed roofing shingles. She saw a tortoise and wildflowers and mushrooms, and she picked some blueberries and ate them right there. She climbed to one of the highest spots on the Eastern Seaboard, breathless but happy, and looked out over the vistas below.

When Tamika got home that night, with the glow of a sunshiny day about her, she told her mother she wasn't going to be a schoolteacher. She was going to be a ranger—maybe an urban ranger, or maybe a ranger in some distant forest she couldn't yet even imagine. Her mother didn't argue. How could she argue with a girl whose eyes shone in a way they never had before? And so Tamika's mother agreed that the money she had saved for college could go toward a degree in something Tamika wanted.

But that's not the end of the story. Seeing Tamika come alive like that did something to Tamika's mother. She wanted to feel that way, too. And she suddenly realized, when she couldn't live her own dream through Tamika anymore, that she could live it herself. Tamika's mother enrolled in night school the very next semester. She is training to be a first-grade teacher, and she's interning now. Every time a six-year-old learns to read, her heart quickens and she knows what it means to live a life she loves.

The moral, of course, is manifold. For one thing, as parents we can't help but dream of what our children might be, but we need to remember that each child has her own star to follow. We also need to watch out that we don't prescribe a life for her that isn't the one she was born to live. Then, too, we need to curb the tendency to live vicariously through our children. Stage mothers who relentlessly push little girls to perform are a classic example, but many a mother to a lesser degree will attempt to force-feed her daughter some dream that the girl doesn't care about in the least. Most often—and this is the truly important lesson here—that dream is one that the mother in question had for herself but never pursued. Or looking at the situation in a more practical way, many mothers—like Tamika's mother—may be trying to shape lives for their daughters that hold the promise of steady employment and security. Who could blame them for that? Still, there are myriad ways a girl can earn a good living, ways you may never even have heard of. Explore the possibilities with your daughter and give her your blessing if she turns out to take a path that wasn't what you had in mind for her. You'll be enriched by her life as she shares with you her experiences in a realm you never knew existed.

> **Y**ou know why adults are always asking kids what they want to be when they grow up? 'Cause they're looking for ideas.
>
> Paula Poundstone

And once again, don't forget that if there's something you always wanted to do, you can still do it. Short of being a gold-medal gymnast or an astronaut, there's not much a woman can't accomplish even if she's middle-aged. And for that matter, while you can't reach the heights in a physical profession at this stage in your life, you can certainly satisfy your longing by taking an adult beginner class. Why drag an unwilling daughter to classes you wish you were taking yourself? Keep in mind that time flies whether you're having fun or not. Life is meant to be enjoyed. Help your daughter enjoy her life, and help yourself as well.

Activity: I'm Going to Get a Life

This part of your daughter's book should not just be about her career aspirations but about all the aspects of a wonderful life that she might envision for herself, now and in the future. She can put down anything from owning her own horse to seeing her name in the paper to traveling the world to discovering the cure for cancer. In this exercise, nothing is impossible. All her wishes can come true. Of course, she knows that real life is never quite like that, but stretching her imagination will make her spirit supple and strong—and make her brave enough to go for what she *really* wants.

Resource

Women and Work: In Their Own Words, by Maureen Michaelson (Troutdale, OR: Newsage Press, 1994).

10

You Gotta Have a Dream

When Olivia was nine years old, she "adopted" a Cabbage Patch Kid and named her James. (The doll came with a name, but Olivia wasn't the sort to be swayed by anybody else's idea of what her doll ought to be called.) In the little "baby book" that accompanied the doll, Olivia painstakingly filled in answers to all the questions about the doll's favorite foods and activities, and Olivia also wrote the following: "James is named after James Galway, the famous flutist. James likes to listen to him play on the radio. She dreams of being a great flute player when she grows up." That night, tucked in bed and hugging James tight, Olivia whispered, "Someday you're going to play the flute and people will hear you on the radio, James. And someday I'm going to be on television. I'm going to have my own show and it will be about saving the environment. That's my dream and I'm going to make it come true."

That's a big dream for such a small person. But oddly enough, it is little girls who have the audacity to dream big. Big girls lose their nerve. The typical little girl is absolutely certain she could be a movie star if she wanted to, or a scientist like Marie Curie or a singer like Mariah Carey or a political figure like Madeleine Albright. Then, as the years go by, the forces of this culture disabuse her of those notions. Consequently, she lowers her sights and settles for a less lofty dream—if, indeed, she has a dream anymore at all.

That development translates into an enormous waste of human potential. Girls who begin to think they're not capable of accomplishing great things end up stunting their own intellectual growth and squandering their talents. Only if girls keep dreaming big will they have any hope at all of fulfilling the promise of their early years. As parents, grandparents, teachers, aunts, and friends, we have the job of helping them do precisely that. After all, almost any accomplished woman can tell you a story about someone in her life who took a special interest in her future and her dreams. For example, Maxine Waters, the congresswoman from California, talks about a dedicated teacher who went far beyond the call of duty to help Maxine realize her potential. As a result, Maxine emerged from a life of poverty and now fights for economic justice for all people.

Another surefire way to inspire your daughter is to make certain she has plenty of opportunities to read about women of diverse achievements and insofar as possible to see them in action. There's nothing like being in the presence of a woman who is proof positive that big dreams can come true to give a girl a booster shot of self-confidence.

Beyond that, schedule periodic "dream updates" with your daughter. Have her talk about how her dreams have stayed the same and how they may have changed or grown. Encourage her to write about these topics to further reinforce them and to help her clarify her thoughts. After all, the truth is that some of the dreams she had when she was eight or nine may have faded because they were in fact unrealistic—she can't become a commercial pilot if she's nearsighted—and some may have gotten crossed off her list because they lost their appeal for legitimate reasons. Olivia, who, at the age of nine, wanted to have her own TV show about environmental issues

> **M**ama exhorted her children at every opportunity to "jump at de sun." We might not land on the sun, but at least we would get off the ground.
>
> **Zora Neale Hurston**

realized when she was twelve that she was more interested in hands-on work than in being on TV. "When I was a little kid, the women on TV seemed really glamorous," she recalls with a grin. "I kind of grew out of that attitude. I didn't want to have to have my hair and makeup perfect all the time and be in a TV studio for the rest of my life."

Olivia, who is now twenty-two and a government employee doing vegetation surveys in the Pacific Northwest forests, was lucky enough to have parents who kept her talking and dreaming big throughout her adolescence, and they kept listening as well. "We never put down any of the stuff she said she wanted to do," her mother says. "Sometimes it sounded pretty off-the-wall but we didn't want to put a lid on her. We would just nod and say, Oh, that's so interesting, where did you hear about that?"

The idea is to keep your daughter in the habit of thinking about the life she could lead one day without giving herself negative messages such as, "I could never do that. I'm too stupid. I'm just a girl. I'm not really good at anything." However, if you do hear self-effacing comments coming out of her mouth, guard against belittling her feelings by saying such things as, "That's silly!" She feels the way she feels and you can't tell her how she *should* feel. What you *can* do is validate her feelings by saying, "I can understand how you could feel that way. Let's talk about what made you feel so bad about yourself."

By the same token, watch out for Pollyanna pronouncements such as, "You can do anything. Girls can do anything." At the moment when your daughter is putting herself down, nothing seems farther from the truth to her, and in a way, she's right. People can make the most of themselves, but none of us is so gifted as to be able to "do anything." Your daughter instinctively knows that. You're far better off helping her pinpoint her unique strengths and interests so that she will be able to reclaim her confidence—and dare to dream once more.

Activity: Dreams I Want to Make Come True

Have your daughter record the results of your "dream updates," keeping track of how she is growing and changing and gaining focus.

Resource

The Difference: Growing Up Female in America, by Judy Mann (New York: Warner, 1994).

11

You're Made of More
Than Sugar and Spice

Everybody knows the nursery rhyme that goes: "Snips and snails and puppy dog tails / That's what little boys are made of / Sugar and spice and everything nice / That's what little girls are made of." Everyone also knows that while there is a tiny grain of truth in there somewhere, in reality boys and girls are a lot more alike than they are different. Both boys and girls can be ambitious and assertive—traits traditionally thought of as masculine. And both boys and girls can be sensitive, nurturing, and expressive—traits traditionally thought of as feminine. Recent research bears this out. And researchers have a name for the fact that both boys and girls can exercise the feminine and the masculine aspects of their nature: healthy androgyny. The word comes from the Greek "andros" for man and "gyneca" for woman.

As applied to your daughter, this means that you want not only to encourage her to let her traditionally feminine traits blossom but also to support her as she finds in herself the traditionally masculine traits that will help her feel good about herself and succeed in life. Donna, age fourteen, is one girl who displays the kind of mix that makes for a strong spirit and the courage to act. She works as a volunteer at a Head Start program, showing great compassion for the children, but as she puts it: "I also have a killer instinct when I'm on the debate team. I am in your face! We went to the state forensics and I was pumped! We won, no problem. What a great feeling!"

Mary Pipher, in her best-selling book *Reviving Ophelia*, writes that androgynous people have "the ability to act adaptively in any situation regardless of gender role constraints. An androgynous person can comfort a baby or change a tire, cook a meal or chair a meeting. Research has shown that since they are free to act without worrying whether their behavior is feminine or masculine, androgynous adults are the most well adjusted." Pipher goes on to say that she entered adolescence, like most of us, "confident, curious and loud," but that she lost all of that. "Most of my adult experience," she writes, "has been the slow trip back to my preadolescent androgynous personality."

Obviously, what you want to do is to prevent that loss for your daughter so that her adult experience can be a journey forward instead of backward. On a practical level, the way to promote androgyny for your daughter is to make sure she has plenty of chances to learn to do things from both her father and her mother that in an earlier time might have been for boys only. Let her try her hand at building a fire in the fireplace, carving the turkey, changing the oil in the car, putting the snow tires on, pruning the maple tree, cleaning out the gutter, painting the house, laying bricks for a patio, barbecuing the burgers, or replacing a fuse. Encourage her to wear comfortable clothes like jeans or sweats and let her know that it's OK to get some dirt under her fingernails. If she acts squeamish about that, or if she says she doesn't want to hold the snake at the petting zoo or dissect a frog in biology class, don't assume that's just how she is. Assume instead that she has picked up on cultural cues about what it means to be a girl and a woman. Girls are not inherently prissy and prim and timid. They learn to be that way. We have to counteract the messages our daughters get from society—and sometimes even the messages they get from women they love.

One girl, now thirteen, whose parents have always given both her and her brother the opportunity to express healthy androgyny, remembers her grandmother fondly but with a certain amazement: "Nana was a perfect lady," she says. "I admired her and I adored her, but the one thing about her that fascinated me from the time I was a very little girl was her hair net. She always got her hair done once a week, and she was obsessed with keeping every hair in place until her next appointment. She always wore that hair net, and she wouldn't do anything that might mess up her hair. She insisted that the car windows be closed tight so the wind wouldn't blow her hair. And once when we were on vacation, she wouldn't ride in a motorboat with the rest of us. She sat on the shore with her hair net on, watching all the fun. I vowed I would never, ever be like that."

Girls need to be free to let their hair blow in the wind, and they need to be free to let their spirits soar. Teaching your daughter tasks and skills with no gender-based restrictions will go a long way toward giving her that freedom. The real benefit, of course, will not so much be that she will know how to change a tire as it will be that she will have the feeling that there's nothing odd about a girl who wants to go for it in any activity or profession she chooses in life.

Activity: I'm Made of More Than Sugar and Spice

Here is where your daughter can list, in two columns, the things about her that society views as traditionally feminine (I like to take care of little kids; I talk a mile a minute; I like to cook) and the things about her that society sees as traditionally masculine (I have a pet iguana; I like to climb trees; I like kickboxing). She can illustrate this chapter with drawings, photographs, or both.

Resource

Free to Be . . . You and Me/And Free to Be a Family: Stories, Songs and Poems for Children and Adults, created by Marlo Thomas; developed and edited by Christopher Cerf, Carole Hart, Francine Klagburn, Letty Cottin Pogrebin, Mary Rogers, and Marlo Thomas (Philadelphia: Running Press, 1998).

12

Don't Just Hang Out, Do Something!

When Susan was in the ninth grade, school got out at 2:30. Most days, she had no particular plans. She would ride the bus home and let herself into an empty house, just as she had done ever since she was eleven and her mother had decided she was old enough not to need a baby-sitter. Susan tried out for the cheerleading squad once but she didn't make it, and there wasn't much else she was interested in when it came to extracurricular activities. So Susan got into the habit of spending most of her afternoons watching the cartoon channel and eating potato chips.

Then on the weekends, Susan and her friends Megan and Jennifer would talk somebody's parents into driving them to the mall. They'd hang out there along with a lot of the other kids. Mostly they would just wander around or pitch pennies in the fountain or try on clothes and test makeup and perfume samples. They'd have lunch at Burger King and maybe buy some earrings or a tube of lipstick. Toward evening, they'd wait out by the front entrance for their ride home.

Then one day, Megan called Susan and said she'd heard about a keg party that was going to happen that weekend. Carol Morrison's parents were going to be away, and Carol's older brother was going to get the kegs of beer. For $5, you could get a plastic cup and as many refills as you wanted. And there might be some pot, too, Megan said, sending a little frisson of fear and excitement down Susan's spine. . . .

You don't want to hear the end of this story, which is true although the names have been changed. It has to do with alcohol poisoning and a young girl hanging close to death in the local hospital. It also has to do with another girl getting arrested for drunk driving, another girl having unprotected sex, and still another one doing time in a detention center at the tender age of seventeen for drug dealing. And then there's the girl who got drunk and almost drowned in the swimming pool in the spacious backyard of the four-bedroom colonial where Carol Morrison hosted the keg party. All of this took place in an affluent suburb peopled by upper-middle-class families with kids who had entirely too much time on their hands and entirely too little supervision and just plain loving care.

Unfortunately, this tragic tale is far from an isolated incident. A recent government report showed that nine out of ten high-school seniors consume alcohol and that most kids today start drinking at the age of twelve. Eight million seventh and eighth graders drink weekly, and 26% of all seventh to twelfth graders have had five or more drinks in a row.

There are many more studies and many more statistics, but let's not belabor the point. Let's talk solutions. Your daughter may be old enough to baby-sit, but that doesn't mean it's fine to leave her to her own devices most of the time in an empty house. Yes, parents who work outside the home, and single parents in particular, are very busy, but making the effort to get our daughters involved in plenty of responsible, enjoyable, stimulating activities will save time and avoid problems later. Girls who are troubled and in trouble are almost always those who have "nothing to do" and nothing to look forward to. And often these same girls remark that no one made an effort to encourage them or invite them to join activities until they became visible as a result of problem behavior.

Sports, Girl Scouts, the marching band, volunteer work, the debate club—the possibilities for getting involved in groups with active peers and adult leadership are legion. Don't listen to a girl who says she doesn't like any of that stuff. Keep exploring until you find something that captures her imagination and gives her a meaningful way to spend her time. When she finds something to do, she'll meet new people, learn new things, and ultimately, feel her own worth. The alternative is simply not an option.

Activity: Here's Where I Belong

Your daughter can devote these pages in her book to recording information about the clubs she belongs to, and any related events she's involved in. She can put in snapshots, clippings from the local newspaper about her and her group, programs, notes of congratulations from her friends, and so on. As always, this section is expandable as time goes by.

Resource

For prevention materials and services plus information on nationwide programs for young people, contact the National Clearinghouse for Alcohol and Drug Information, P.O. Box 2345, Rockville, MD 20847-2345; 800-729-6686; TDD 800-487-4889; (web site) http://www.health.org/gpower.

13

A Dead End Is Not the End of the World

The psychological concept of resilience has to do with a person's ability to withstand and deal successfully with stress and disappointment. As such, it is a characteristic that adolescent girls sorely need to develop. Research has shown that at least one-third of adolescent girls experience feelings of depression. Also, a study done by Susan Nolen-Hoeksema at Stanford University showed that girls are almost twice as prone to depression as boys are.

Why? Anne C. Petersen, Ph.D., deputy director of the National Science Foundation, maintains that there is a "gender pattern that women are much more realistic about situations." She goes on to say, however, "We can't let knowing and being realistic about situations be so overwhelming that we get incapacitated and then can't think about how to transform it." That is why, according to Suzanne Ouellette, Ph.D., resilience means more than just the capacity to "bounce back." Rather, resilient people are capable of *transforming* stressful situations, even as they refuse to succumb to depression and hopelessness. On a personal level, that means speaking up about something that's not fair—a final grade calculated without regard to work done for extra credit or a penalty called by a referee who didn't see what really happened. And on a grander scale, that means working to change injustice in society.

As Dr. Ouellette put it: "If depression is linked to stressful life events, then you need to go in and change the situation in which those events are happening." That is a very exciting concept. Share it with your daughter and see if she's moved by it enough to want to become what academicians call an "agent for social change." If so, encourage her to work in conjunction with others for a cause she believes in—organizing against drunk driving, making sure her school supports girls' athletic events, starting an after-school self-defense class. A girl who feels she really has the power to do something about the world's problems, particularly as they affect her own life, is going to have a lot more inner strength when it comes to dealing with all problems.

However, along with that psychological strength, you can also arm your daughter with coping skills that will keep her from falling prey to depression. Charles R. Snyder, Ph.D., a psychologist at the University of Kansas in Lawrence, has done extensive research on what he calls "high hope" people, and he has concluded that they see life as a kind of maze or game board. "When they hit a dead end, they don't see it as the end of the world. They simply turn around and look for another way," he says. "Or if they feel like they're losing the game, they don't give up. They see the situation as a challenge and they think up another strategy."

> **It is the duty of youth to bring its fresh new powers to bear on social progress. Each generation of young people should be to the world like a vast reserve force to a tired army. They should lift the world forward.**
>
> **That is what they are for.**
>
> Charlotte Perkins Gilman

Try this exercise with your daughter. Draw a maze. Brainstorm with her about what labels you could put on some of the dead ends. Have her imagine what events have made or would make her sad or discouraged or disappointed. She might come up with "Breaking up with Brad" or "Not bringing my social studies grade up" or "Not making the basketball team" or "Not getting a part in the school play" or "Not getting to take karate lessons because my mom got laid off."

Remember that whatever your daughter is experiencing is a very big deal to her. Don't say something like "A lot of people are a lot worse off than you are" or "Ten years from now it won't matter whether you were in the school play." Take her seriously. Talk about the dead ends and help her find another way out of the maze. Discuss paths that might lead to freedom and feeling good. Being dumped by Brad hurts, but it doesn't mean she'll never have another boyfriend. And while she's between relationships, she might just have more energy and time for her other interests. Also, remind her of Little Orphan Annie warbling with relentless cheer that "The sun'll come out tomorrow!" No matter what we do, there will always be dark days and bright days. High hope people see this as a simple—if somewhat regrettable—fact of life. They don't indulge in self-blame or self-pity. "People who are high on cognitive energy definitely carry on an inner dialogue about their ability to succeed," says Snyder. "If they do fail, they tell themselves they tried the wrong tack or that life is sometimes like that and you have to take your share of lumps."

Finally, you can remind your daughter that the sun really will come out tomorrow, or at least sometime soon. Also, by supporting your daughter in her efforts to change situations that are oppressive, you'll be arming her against despair. And don't forget to tell her you love her and you'll always be there for her even when you seem too busy. Then be sure you keep your promise. No business meeting, no deadline, no client is as important as your daughter when she needs you.

Activity: I Can Change the World!

For this chapter in her book, have your daughter make a list of things that aren't fair, both in her personal life and in the world in general. Help her out by pointing her to newspaper articles that talk about social issues. Have her collect clippings and keep them in the pocket folders. Then have her arrange her items into two groups: WHAT I HAVE TO ACCEPT (I'm too tall to be a gymnast; I'm hearing-impaired; a lot of virgin forest land has already been logged) and WHAT I CAN CHANGE (my math grade; the fact that there aren't any girls running for class president; the fact that women get paid less than men for the same work). This list is the beginning of an ongoing project, and she should come back to it

> **D**on't agonize. Organize.
>
> Florynce R. Kennedy

with periodic updates—a note that she got a B+ in math, or a report that she and a group of her friends have banded together to help a girl run for class president, or a collection of newspaper clippings about equal pay for equal work. She might also like to put in her book this quote from Helen Keller, a woman of great achievement in spite of the fact that she was both blind and deaf: "No pessimist ever discovered the secrets of stars, or sailed to an uncharted land, or opened a new heaven to the human spirit."

Resources

A Parents' Guide for Suicidal and Depressed Teens: Help for Recognizing If a Child Is in Crisis and What to Do About It, by Kate Williams (Center City, MN: Hazelden Foundation, 1995).

Understanding Your Teenager's Depression, by Kathleen McCoy, Ph.D. (New York: Perigee, 1994).

14

Don't Bang Your Head Against a Brick Wall

Tara Lipinski, the teenage skating sensation, was in Manhattan signing autographs for scores of adoring fans at Macy's. Most of the fans were girls ten and eleven years old, and most of them were skaters, young hopefuls with dreams of landing a triple lutz with the same precision and pizzazz that Tara displays, and maybe even of becoming a world champion someday. Among those fans was a girl named Katie, a bright-eyed kid with a quirky grin and a headful of red ringlets. She stood several inches taller than most of the other girls in the crowd even though she had just turned ten. A passerby asked her whether she took skating lessons.

"Yeah, and I'm not very good at it," she said with her lopsided smile and a twinkle in her eye. "I like it, though. My mom lets me do it because she knows I have fun and it's good for my coordination. I take gymnastics, too, and I'm not very good at that either." Charmed by this self-assured child, the passerby asked a few more questions and learned that Katie had been reading since she was four, that she is good at math, and that she thinks she probably wants to be an engineer like her father. "Some of the kids in my skating class are so into it, like they want to be Tara or something. But that is so dumb, unless they're good at it. My mom talked to me about that. She said everybody's got different things they're good at. She says it's fine to try hard but it's stupid to bang your head against a brick wall. I wasn't cut out to be a skater but I don't care."

Katie's mother has given her very good advice. She has let her daughter know that persistence alone doesn't always make dreams come true. Everybody has limitations. Yet each of us can find the way to her personal best, as long as she doesn't waste time banging her head against a wall. If your daughter is challenged in some way, or if she wasn't born to excel in certain careers, your job is to get her to avoid dwelling on her weaknesses and start celebrating her strengths. Acknowledge the fact that life is not always fair, and move on from there. Also, enlist the help of mentors. Harvard scholar Robert Coles looked at children who succeeded against overwhelming odds and coined the term "invulnerables" to describe them. His work showed that the most resilient young people are those who report a sense of caring and connectedness with at least one competent adult, not necessarily the child's parent. Results of the Minnesota Adolescent Health Survey also show the importance of the role of at least one caring adult in promoting resilience in a young person. The more people who love your daughter and guide her toward a goal she can realistically reach, the better.

Alicia Howard, a thirteen-year-old visually impaired girl who was born in Indiana, is a case in point. At the age of four, she was diagnosed with a rare eye disease that caused a thinning of her corneas. As a result of the condition, Alicia's corneas tore in both eyes, requiring emergency surgery by specialists in Chicago. But she is fortunate enough to have a devoted aunt, Shelly J. Tucciarelli, who lives in Chicago and who took Alicia under her wing. Alicia's father and brother remained in Indiana and her mother commuted back and forth, but Alicia's aunt made sure Alicia didn't give in to despair. Alicia made up her mind that even though there were many jobs she wouldn't be able to consider— and even though ordinary skills like driving a car would never be hers— she would make a life for herself. She has started doing all she can to get a good education. In the Chicago public school system, Alicia is in a class for visually impaired students half of the day and in a regular classroom the other half of the day. She also has a mobility teacher who takes her class out in the Chicago neighborhoods so they can learn how to cross streets and walk around the city safely. Because of her Native American heritage, Alicia qualifies for a Bureau of Indian Affairs college grant and she is eagerly looking forward to going to college. Wisely, she is focusing not on what she *can't* do but on what she *can* do. In the words of Sojourner Truth, an early black feminist, "What don't kill me make me strong." That is a lesson for us all.

Activity: I'm Doing What I Do Best

If your daughter has a learning disability or a physical challenge, have her write about that and consider turning it around so that it strengthens her. She may be inspired to become a specialist in the field she already knows so well. Perhaps she could be a tutor with a real sensitivity to dyslexic children's needs, or she could become a physical therapist or a surgeon. Or have her explore life options that utilize her strengths and bypass her limitations.

If your daughter is not physically challenged but is simply, like all of us, not cut out for certain occupations, have her look for ones she's well suited for. She can collect pictures, do some research in the library, and interview people in the fields that pique her interest.

Resource

Educational Equity Concepts, 114 E. 32nd Street, Suite 701, New York, NY 10016; 212-725-1803 (voice/TTY).

15

Dream Possible Dreams

You want your daughter to set her goals high, but you don't want her to waste time tilting at windmills. Dreaming the impossible dream has an inspiring sound to it at first, but if you think again, you'll realize that it's simply not a good plan. Listen to eighteen-year-old Nicole Loskutoff of San Rafael, California, a girl who looked at her abilities and personality with a cold eye and ended up with a possible dream.

"I joined the jazz band my freshman year. Jazz became a new world for me to explore, and I soon realized that it was one of my greatest loves. But I also knew that I had neither the dedication nor the discipline to become a successful musician. I feared that I would lose the music if I did not become a musician, so I developed the goal that somehow I would find a way to make sure that the music did not escape my life entirely.

"During the past year I have had opportunities I previously thought to be inaccessible for someone my age. Through an internship obtained as a result of attending Take Our Daughters to Work day last year at Carlos Santana's management office, I discovered my true place in the world. The night I attended one of Carlos' shows, I had what one may call an epiphany. I realized what I wanted to focus my life on and how I could use everything my mentors had taught me and inspired within me. I have developed a passionate interest in sound engineering during my internship. Working in a studio as a recording engineer would allow me to remain close to the music."

The lesson Nicole exemplifies is an important one. We have already explored the fact that people have limitations and disabilities, but Nicole's story introduces another factor. She says with arresting candor that she has "neither the dedication nor the discipline to become a successful musician." Notice that she does not say she has no talent. She is simply assessing with ruthless honesty her own makeup. She is not kicking herself or being judgmental. And as a result she is able to retain a full measure of self-worth and go forward in an aspect of the music business that she feels is suited to her personality.

> **N**ever underestimate the ability of a small, dedicated group of people to change the world; indeed, it's the only thing that ever has.
>
> **Margaret Mead**

This is a commendable accomplishment in a culture that keeps pounding home the idea that people can "do anything." Walk into any card shop and you'll see posters and pins, meant to be inspirational, that bear such slogans as "Believe in yourself, and all things are possible." Every girl knows in her heart that that is not true. Believing doesn't make basketball superstars or concert pianists or Nobel Prize winners or presidents or much of anything, really. What's needed is just the right combination of talent and drive and support—and opportunity. For girls, especially, that last ingredient often remains elusive. Yet when it is supplied, the results can be wonderful. As Nicole put it: "The kindness of all who work at the office has given me the strength to believe I can achieve my dream. I have gained a lifetime of confidence because of their faith in me and all I have been taught. If every young girl is given the opportunity and trust to explore her interests as I have, that is the best gift she can receive."

We know that you are making every effort to see that your daughter receives that gift, and that she has every chance to find her possible dream and work toward making it come true.

Activity: I Know About a Lot of Possibilities

Have your daughter make two columns on a piece of filler paper. In the left column, she should write a list of general occupational categories or fields, leaving five or ten lines between each entry. Examples might be medicine, law, the arts, science, entertainment, communication, education, government, sports, and so on. Then in the right column, she can list specific jobs pertaining to each field of endeavor. She can start with her wildest dreams (president of the United States for "government," WNBA superstar for "sports," Academy Award–winning actor for "entertainment") and then write down other jobs in that field. Help her do some research for this, and encourage her to interview people in several fields. She might come up with speechwriter for "government," sportscaster for "sports," and stage manager for "entertainment." The point is for her to discover the myriad ways she could be involved in any given field and make the best use of her talents. She may realize that she would really rather be a sportscaster than a basketball superstar even if she has the potential for the latter. Examined at close range, the most "visible" and "glamorous" jobs are not always the most appealing after all.

Resource

Wishcraft: How to Get What You Really Want, by Barbara Sher with Annie Gottlieb (New York: Ballantine Books, 1984).

16

Expect the Unexpected

Parades get rained on, parties get canceled, promises get broken, plans get changed, stuff gets lost, accidents happen. Life is full of surprises—some of them pleasant, but a great many of them not so pleasant and plenty of them downright awful. Successful people understand that. They are organized and they plan ahead, but they are not amazed when plans go awry. If they get knocked down, they pick themselves up, dust themselves off, and start all over again.

For a young girl buffeted by the storm of female adolescence, however, maintaining that kind of emotional buoyancy is most often not easy. You can help by setting a good example and not letting yourself be thrown by day-to-day upsets. Even so, the small stuff can seem pretty big to a teenage girl, as Rachel, age thirteen, demonstrates: One evening, she collapsed on her bed in tears and wouldn't come down to dinner. Her mother went in and rubbed Rachel's back in silence for a while. When the sobbing had subsided somewhat, Rachel's mother asked her if she wanted to talk. "It's just one thing after another," Rachel said, sitting up and blowing her nose. "I went for math extra help every day last week—I even skipped lacrosse practice—and I was so sure I was going to ace the math test, but I still only got a B minus. Then the lacrosse coach threatened to suspend me for cutting practice! So I wanted to tell Ginny, who is supposedly my best friend, but she sat with this girl Marisa at lunch and totally ignored me. I was mortified. They were whispering and laughing, and I know they were talking about me. Then when I got home there was an e-mail saying my baby-sitting job for tomorrow is canceled. Great! I, like, already spent the money! Nothing ever goes right. I'm a total loser!"

What Rachel and other girls like her need is to realize that things never settle down. She needs to learn how to reach inside herself and find a wellspring of strength. Two ways to help your daughter find the reservoir within herself and get it to flow include yoga and meditation, the age-old paths to serenity. Look for courses in your area, as well as spas or resorts. Or you can learn the techniques employed by spas and apply them at home. That way, when life throws some unexpected punches, both you and your daughter will be far better able to roll with them.

There is a wonderful book called *The Wellness Center's Spa at Home,* by Kalia Doner and Margaret Doner, L.M.T. The authors give instructions on how to create stress-reducing spa experiences with simple, affordable supplies right in your own home. You and your daughter can try out recipes for herbal soaks, aromatherapy, natural facials, body wraps, scrubs, massages, stretching and toning routines, and nutritious eating regimens. Most important, there is a chapter on guided meditation that takes the hocus-pocus out of this tension-easing skill. Some of the meditations require no more than five minutes, but they work wonders. By sharing all of this with your daughter, you'll be accomplishing two important goals. First, you'll be arming her with healthy ways to combat stress, fatigue, confusion, and anxiety so that she will be much less likely to resort to such ill-advised sources of relief as drugs, smoking, alcohol, eating disorders, and self-mutilation. And second, by taking the time to soothe your own spirit, you'll be setting an excellent example and showing your daughter that even a woman as busy as you are values herself enough to treat herself well.

In addition, teach your daughter the importance of the following three approaches to life, distilled from the current literature and thinking on maintaining emotional equanimity and a sense of serenity:

1) *Make the most of every moment.* Mastering the art of focusing on each instant as you live it—getting the juice out of it, and not wasting time feeling sorry for yourself or wishing your life away—is an invaluable self-esteem booster. You want your daughter to plan ahead and look forward to the future, but don't let her get so involved in the stress of scoring high on the SATs that she misses the miracle of living fully in the here and now.

2) *Don't be afraid of change.* Serene is not the same as static. Encourage your daughter to get up, get out, and go for it. If she never takes any chances or tries anything new, she could end up treading water for the rest of her life.

3) *Stop waiting for the pieces of your life to fall into place.* Your daughter needs to think of life not as a puzzle to be finished and then preserved, but as a game board, requiring strategies and a glorious sense of adventure. In other words, life is not a destination but a journey. We never really "get there" and things never really "settle down." Life is, as Rachel put it, "just one thing after another," but the trick is to see that fact as natural and even positive, not as discouraging and defeating.

Activity: I Know Healthy Ways to Make Myself Feel Better

Have your daughter list some of the things she learned from your spa-at-home activities, and list her personal favorites (the scent of lavender for aromatherapy; chamomile tea both as a calming drink and as an herbal soak; a CD with the sound of waves breaking on the beach; a five-minute meditation that works for her).

Resource

Peace Is Every Step: The Path of Mindfulness in Everyday Life, by Thich Nhat Hanh (New York: Bantam, 1992).

17

Different Is Good

When she was seven years old, with that sky-is-the-limit spirit so typical of little girls, Lisa-Brett Scott announced that she wanted to be a choreographer. She was a student at the Huntington School of Ballet on Long Island, and she had done her share of *Nutcracker* performances as an angel and a girl in the party scene, but Lisa-Brett wanted to do something more important than learn steps and wear a pretty costume. So when Black History Month rolled around, Lisa—who is the daughter of an African-American father and a Caucasian mother—corralled some of her fellow dance students. With a little help from their teacher, Lisa-Brett created a ballet entitled *Skin Deep*.

As the ballet opens, two Caucasian boys and a Caucasian girl are dancing and playing hide-and-seek to the cheery strains of an Offenbach galop. Suddenly, that music ends and the powerful first chord of Aaron Copland's "Theme for a Common Man" startles the children, as does the entrance of Lisa-Brett, the biracial child. On the next chord, a Korean girl appears. The ballet goes on to explore themes of rejection, fear, and struggle, until at last the children realize that they are all the same inside. They reach across an imaginary barrier and clasp hands, forming a final tableau of trust and tolerance.

Lisa-Brett's mother did the paperwork required to enter this remarkable ballet in the state-sponsored Martin Luther King, Jr., contest for young artists. The little troupe of dancers was invited to Albany, the state capital, to perform the ballet. Lisa-Brett, the seven-year-old choreographer, won first place in her age category.

> **I** didn't belong as a kid and that always bothered me. If only I'd known that one day my differences would be an asset, then my early life would have been much easier.
>
> **Bette Midler**

Back home, Lisa-Brett appeared on a segment of Long Island's News Channel 12. The caption under her read "award-winning choreographer." The reporter who interviewed her asked Lisa-Brett what her ballet was about and she said, "It's about how people can be good friends regardless of their color and how everyone deserves respect."

That early experience of creating a work of art and expressing a positive multicultural message stayed with Lisa-Brett as she entered the perilous passage from girlhood to womanhood. Now fifteen, Lisa-Brett is vice president of the Leaders Club in her town, an organization of young people working to promote positive lifestyles for youth and to do community service. As for her experience as a seven-year-old, she has this to say: "I think doing something so mature when I was so young helped keep me on an even keel and made me determined to keep achieving and doing things I believe in." Lisa-Brett also stresses that creating the ballet gave her a strong sense that it's OK to be different. "I'm allowed to date now, and I've had two African-American boyfriends and one Caucasian. I have friends of every race, and we all care about each other and support each other."

We all know that being different in adolescence can be painful, but in a certain way, girls who can't fit this society's stereotype for perfection (most often translated as white, blond, and beautiful) have an advantage. They aren't as likely to be pulled into the perfect girls' world and can use their "outsider edge" to make themselves stronger—and to make the world a better place. We need to help them appreciate the power of sharing the special perspective that difference gives them.

In fact, research and experience have both shown that being different can prove to be a source of strength. Girls with a difference are often the first to get involved in programs for social change in order to better the lives of all people, and that very act of working to effect change gives them the psychological resilience we talked about earlier. They gain strength by transforming a source of stress or an injustice instead of buckling under in the face of it. Qiana O'Bryant, an eighteen-year-old African-American girl, is a perfect example. "I participated in Take Our Daughters to Work day for three consecutive years; beginning in 1994," Qiana wrote. "My mentor for each year was a woman by the name of Ms. Sandra Harris. When we met, she worked as a general manager for the Chicago Housing Authority. Ms. Harris helped me get a good start. She encouraged me to set goals, stay focused, and work hard." Qiana followed that advice and was eventually elected president of the youth committee in her community. As a result, she was invited to go to Washington, D.C., in May 1996 to represent the Chicago Housing Authority at the First Annual National Meeting Youth Conference. "My being in Washington made me feel like I could do anything," Qiana reports. "So I ran for president of the National Association of Resident Management Corporation Youth Council and of course I won. I was also involved in what was called a 'mock trial.' This was an exercise where youth tried a fictional court case involving troubled girls." Qiana has plans to go to college and she concludes by saying, "The world is my oyster!"

Activity: "What's the Difference?"

Encourage your daughter to find pen pals whose heritages, cultures, and lifestyles are different from hers. The Girl Scouts of the U.S.A. has a Pen Pal Network that links troops together so that girls can correspond with other Girl Scouts in a different part of the country. This Pen Pal program is currently open to registered Girl Scout troops and groups at the Brownie, Junior, Cadette, and Senior Girl Scout levels. Write to Girl Scouts of the U.S.A., 450 Fifth Avenue, New York, NY 10018-2702.

Here are some tips for writing to pen pals that you can share with your daughter:

Tell your pen pals about yourself, your family, your mentors, your home, your friends, your community activities, your leaders, your neighborhood, your school, your town, your special holidays and customs, your career aspirations, any sports you're involved in, any clubs you belong to, any offices you hold. Ask your pen pals questions about all of these same areas and exchange snapshots, sketches, and maps.

Your daughter's correspondence and memorabilia from her pen pals can go in this chapter of her book.

Resources

Lisa-Brett Scott recommends *Listen Up: Voices from the Next Feminist Generation*, edited by Barbara Findlen (Seattle, WA: Seal Press, 1995).

New Moon, a bimonthly magazine for girls that fosters multicultural understanding; 800-381-4743; (web site) http://www.newmoon.org.

18

You Can Chart Your Own Course

W hat a girl needs as she leaves childhood and makes the passage to adulthood is to feel that she is capable of becoming a self-reliant person with a clear sense of direction. Being self-reliant, however, does not mean acting alone. The surest way to help your daughter find her way is to make certain she has plenty of opportunities right now to feel that she's valuable and that people are interested in her and ready to lend a hand. As we have said in another context, that is one of the main benefits of Take Our Daughters to Work day, and one of the most important lessons to extract from the day and inject into your daughter's life every day. Yes, learning about work options is important. But learning that adults are vitally interested in the lives of girls is more important still. Listen to these confident voices of girls who have been welcomed into the world of work and thereby gained a belief that they can chart a course and get themselves where they want to go:

"I have learned from Take Our Daughters to Work day that I am just as free and smart as any male or female out there. I can do what I want and succeed. I can be proud to be a woman in the twenty-first century. I have learned to set standards for myself and

strive to meet them. I also know that if I can't meet all my goals, I won't be discouraged. I'll be proud of myself and my generation."

Shannon Scott, Augusta, Maine, age fourteen

"I was able to go with my mom, who currently works for Washington State Patrol. When I was with my mom, one of the things that I learned was that you can do anything you want. I found that this is true in everything you do and not only in school. An example that happened to me was in sports. When I was in seventh grade, I didn't make the volleyball team. I really loved to play so I chose to go to camp all summer to improve my skills. In eighth grade I made the team. Now, in ninth grade as a freshman, I made the junior varsity team and we had an undefeated season."

Melissa Kirkeby, Olympia, Washington, age fifteen

"Carol Jenkins, a former anchorwoman at NBC News here in New York, invited me to spend the day with her at the news station. We went out into the streets accompanied by a camera crew, and interviewed people with girls about their plans for the day. It made me feel strong to see other girls taking charge inside the workplace and letting adults know that we are ready to lead. I learned that being a girl is a wonderful thing, something to be proud of, and we deserve to be treated with respect.

"I currently produce a cable talk show called *Youth Forum*, devoted to tackling real issues concerning girls, and our struggles in society. I don't have to accept things the way they are, I have the power to change them. Take Our Daughters to Work day has provided me with an inner strength that will carry me into womanhood."

Jasmine Victoria, New York, New York, age sixteen

If ever there were proof of how the lessons of one day can become the lessons of a lifetime, these stories are it. For these girls, the event was much, much more than just a "career day." The day gave them the strength and drive to steer unerringly toward their goals and make a difference as well. Why not share their stirring testimonies with your daughter? Then arrange for her to go to work with you or someone else and encourage her to talk about her experiences. Go on from there to explore with her ways she might apply the lessons of one day to her life every day, now and in the future.

Activity: I'm Steering Straight for Success

Have your daughter glue together four pieces of plain filler paper and fold them accordion-style so they'll fit into her notebook. Then have her unfold them and draw a winding "river." You can work together with her to "chart her course." Have her draw in some danger zones—white-water rapids, a waterfall, rocks, etc.—and name them with real-life dangers that could get her off course, such as an unwanted pregnancy, dropping out of school, or doing drugs. Now come up with solutions—a helping hand from someone who cares, staying in sports, taking her schoolwork seriously, and so on. If you're really creative, you can turn this into a board game patterned after such childhood classics as Chutes and Ladders and Candyland.

Resource

Don't Stop Loving Me: A Reassuring Guide for Mothers of Adolescent Daughters, by Ann E. Caron (New York: Henry Holt, 1992).

Part Two

Explore Your Options

19

Ask for Help

The word *mentor*, currently defined as "wise and trusted counselor," comes from Greek mythology. Mentor was Odysseus's trusted counselor, and it was in Mentor's disguise that Athena became the guardian and counselor of Odysseus's son Telemachus in his father's absence. Our work has shown that having a mentor is a great benefit when it comes to supporting or raising a girl's aspirations. Think of your own life. If you're like most of us, you can point to a teacher, a friend of the family, a friend's mother—someone who fired your imagination and ambition. And if you were lucky enough to build a solid relationship with that person, you were helped over time by knowing she believed in your potential. Listen to the astonishing story of Whitney P. Rogers, age sixteen, who took the initiative and got herself not one, but two mentors to help her in her quest to become an astronaut:

In April of 1996, I heard a guest lecture, and something magic happened. Here was a female test pilot—a woman actually taking the career path that I had always dreamed of following! Her story opened with memories of how the world had held her back. Women were not supposed to be test pilots; it was much too dangerous, much too com-

plicated. "But I refused to face those facts," she exclaimed. "I became a test pilot! I'm living my dream and you can live yours, provided you don't wait for someone to hand you the opportunity. Go out and create it for yourself. Take responsibility for building your own future."

I immediately tried her advice. At the end of her presentation, I went up to the front of the auditorium introduced myself, thanked her for coming, and asked for her address. I wrote her a letter, not really expecting an answer. Surprise—she wrote back!

A year later, I saw a profile in the newspaper of a woman who was the director of the Mars Program at a nearby NASA center. I took the initiative and wrote to her. Surprise!—she e-mailed back to me! So, as a result, in a few weeks I am going to visit the NASA center and meet my new mentor as a part of the 1997 Take Our Daughters to Work day.

If I could give a message to every girl in the world, it would be this: Never wait for an opening to be presented to you, but take responsibility for making your own dreams come true.

Just a few weeks ago, I was able to meet Dr. Sally Ride, the first American woman in space, and my hero. With the advice of my test pilot mentor echoing in my ears, I asked for her address, and wrote her a letter that same day. I'm waiting to hear.

Will she write back?

Whitney's story is inspiring, and there are many, many others like it. In fact, very often a mentor becomes an ally over time. That's exactly what happened for seventeen-year-old Leah Scherzer, who first shadowed Dr. Janet Stein, an obstetrician at Beth Israel Hospital in New York, in 1995. Leah has this to say: "The relationship that I formed with her is a continuing one. I encourage every girl to participate in this activity because hopefully it won't only be a one-day opportunity but the start of a long-lasting relationship."

Activity: I Know How to Ask the Right Questions

Interviewing a mentor takes some preparation. Brainstorm with your daughter about the things she might ask. What did you study in school? Did you have a mentor yourself? Were you inspired by any books? Do you have family responsibilities? How do you balance work and family life? What did you dream of when you were my age? Did any of your dreams come true? Did you change your mind about some of your dreams? What courses would you recommend for me to take in school if I want to follow in your footsteps? You and your daughter can come up with many more questions, some of them pertaining to the specific job her mentor has and many having to do with life in general.

You may also want to use a tape recorder and have your daughter do some practice interviews

> **T**he thing women have got to learn is that nobody gives you power. You just take it.
>
> **Roseanne**

with you, pretending she wants to follow your career path and have you as a mentor. Then reverse the procedure so that you are interviewing her about some aspect of her life such as her club or sports activities. Now when you play the tapes back, listen not only for grammar goofs and slang but also for "ums" and "ahs" and other fillers such as "You know what I mean?" Then try the interviews again and see how she improves. (You'll probably end up sharpening your own oral skills while you're helping your daughter with hers!)

Along with her speech habits, your daughter also needs to pay attention to how she presents herself visually when she meets her mentor so that she will feel comfortable in her new setting. A lot of girls solve the problem of what to wear by getting one of the T-shirts with the Take Our Daughters to Work day logo. This levels the playing field and takes the focus off of who has the coolest outfit.

Finally, make sure your daughter understands the value of her mentor's time. She needs to arrive when she's expected for appointments. She also needs to thank her mentor and write a follow-up thank-you note. That's not only proper etiquette—it's good networking!

Resource

For All Our Daughters, by Pegine Echevarria (Worcester, MA: Chandler House Press, 1998).

20

Beyond the "Picket Fence"

During the 1950s, when the prevailing sentiments in this country were "I Love Lucy" and "I Like Ike," a historical aberration—the one-job, two-parent nuclear family in a single-family home—became the norm for the first time ever. Yet the trend that started with postwar prosperity abetted by the G.I. Bill eventually came to be regarded as "traditional." In truth, however, that Donna Reed vision of a happy homemaker in a shirtwaist and pearls cheerily waving good-bye to her husband in a gray flannel suit was an anomaly in our social history.

Stephanie Coontz, in *The Way We Never Were: American Families and the Nostalgia Trap*, points out that neither the 1950s nor any other period provides a workable model of how to structure our family lives today. Similarly, political analyst Kevin Phillips documented in *Boiling Point* that plenty of eighteenth- and nineteenth-century women worked, whether on the farm or in mom-and-pop shops or as teachers. True, there were not a lot of women in high-ranking positions in the business or industrial worlds, and if women were in those arenas at all, they were in sweatshops. That's the inequity that the women's movement was dedicated to correcting, right along with the injustice that the more privileged women of that time suffered by being mere chattel without suffrage. But at least those women had a support system in the form of the extended family. The postwar phenomenon, on the other hand, not only put the whole burden of providing for the family on the man while sending Rosie the Riveter home again after she had already proved her mettle in the outside world, but it also cloistered Mom, Dad, and the kids away from the grandparents. The result was that the vine-covered cottage surrounded by a white picket fence ended up putting women right back into the position of being economic captives. Nineteenth-century feminist Charlotte Perkins Gilman evoked the helplessness of that position in this passage from a clever story about a woman who turns into a man: "All at once, with a deep rushing sense of power and pride, she felt what she had never felt before in all her life—the possession of money, of her own earned money—hers to give or to withhold, not to beg for, tease for, wheedle for—hers."

That rushing sense of power and pride that earning money brings is probably in the future for all our daughters. Today, girls know that their lives will include work inside and outside the proverbial picket fence. A 1994 New York Times/CBS News poll with boys and girls showed that 86% of girls expect to work and 81% of boys expect that their wives will work.

Girls also know that the world of work offers rewards both tangible and intangible to help them become fully realized human beings. For Adrienne Hagedorn, a sixteen-year-old girl from Morgantown, West Virginia, that truth became clear over the course of three years during which she was lucky enough to participate in Take Our Daughters to Work day. Adrienne's mother is a secretary in the office of student activities at West Virginia University, and Adrienne writes: "Last year was especially memorable. The day offered a panel discussion that had women within the university who held what they considered 'nontraditional' roles: director of news services, girls' basketball coach, police officer, and minister. It was a great chance to hear and learn some of the challenges they had faced getting to their positions and how they dealt with them. They all emphasized the importance of females setting high goals."

Adrienne goes on to say that her grandmother, a "traditional" homemaker, once told her that "the reason the world was in the condition it was is that we let women have too much power." As a result of her exposure to women of achievement in nontraditional roles, Adrienne heartily disagrees with her grandmother. "I will show her that women can make a difference, a good, productive, valuable contribution to the world," Adrienne states unequivocally.

To help your own daughter garner that same sense of purpose, be sure she sees strong women in action. Also talk with her about women who have made a difference. A wonderful resource to share with your teenager is *Herstory: Women Who Changed the World*, by Ruth Ashby and Deborah Gore Ohrn. You'll find 120 inspiring biographical sketches of women from ancient times to the present, ranging from Queen Hatshepsut to Rigoberta Menchú. For a younger daughter, see the Women of Achievement biography series published by Chelsea House in New York.

Reading aloud with your daughter is the very best way to make the lessons in the books stick. Remember how cozy and intimate those moments used to be as you read bedtime stories to her when she was a little girl? Make an effort to recapture that closeness by taking turns reading aloud to each other. She may say she'd rather talk on the phone with her friends or watch TV, and for that matter, you may think you're too drained after a day at the office to feel like interacting with her. But try it. Start with just a twenty-minute session. You'll be surprised how your energy returns when a certain story of dedication and dreams coming true lights up her eyes. And yours.

Activity: I Admire Women Who Went Down in History

This is similar to the first chapter in your daughter's book when she listed contemporary role models. Again, have her make two columns, the one on the right for names and the one on the left for attributes and accomplishments. She can list famous women as well as women from her family—grandmothers, great-aunts, great-grandmothers. This might also be a good time to suggest that she go back to her list in the first chapter and see if she wants to make some changes based on all that she has been learning about herself, about girls in general, about women's lives, and about our culture.

Resource

"Women Who Dare," an engagement calendar published every year by the Library of Congress. Scores of inspiring stories, plus a notation for each day.

Take Our Daughters to Work day trading cards. To order, call 800-676-7780; (web site) http://www.ms.foundation.org.

21

Go Off in Two (or More) Directions at Once

The fork-in-the-road metaphor is inevitably evoked when a discussion of finding one's path in life comes up. That's unfortunate, because it precludes the very real possibility that someone—your daughter?—may have the talents and desires to achieve in two or more professions at the same time or in tandem throughout her lifetime. True, when we literally come to a fork in a road, we do indeed have to make a choice. We turn either right or left, and the other way becomes the road not taken. But when we come to a point in life where we figuratively have two possible ways to go, it's entirely conceivable that we could follow both and thus not risk looking back with regret about aspirations that never flowered because they were nipped in the bud. Think about Agnes de Mille, the choreographer who brought ballet to Broadway in 1943 with the immensely popular dream sequence in the musical *Oklahoma!* De Mille was also a dancer herself, portraying most notably the Cowgirl in her ballet *Rodeo.* And she was a gifted writer, producing eleven books, including the perennial favorite *Dance to the Piper* and *Portrait Gallery,* the critically acclaimed book of biographical sketches that she wrote at the age of eighty-five, just a year before her death in 1993. Then there is Eugenia Zuckerman, a flutist and a novelist, and plenty of other less well-known women who fit the dictionary definition of a Renaissance woman: "A woman who has broad intellectual interests and is accomplished in areas of both the arts and the sciences."

The point here is that if your daughter shows a range of interests and aptitudes, there's no need to narrow her field of potential pursuits. Certainly, it's important for her not to spread herself too thin and not to take on so much that she becomes a Jill-of-all-trades and master of none. But if she has a knack for horticulture and a passion for politics, there's no reason one of those has to be forgone or even relegated to avocational status. Why couldn't she end up operating a home-based greenhouse business—and also run for office? In fact, instead of distracting her, the combination of one essentially right-brained activity with one left-brained career would probably keep her from burning out in either area.

In a similar vein, people often start in one direction and stop and try another. Most adults have actually had several jobs. Interviewing people about this can be reassuring for your daughter if she has the somewhat scary notion that she has to choose one life path early on and stick to it. Making a midcourse correction or trying a new direction altogether is not the same as being a quitter at all. Almost always, the knowledge and experience gained from one venture will be useful in the next. A theater studies major who learns about budgeting could end up using those skills if she decides later on to work for a not-for-profit agency. A girl who starts out majoring in Spanish and then decides she'd rather be a math teacher may end up with a choice spot as a bilingual educator. A girl who wants to be both a poet and a physician might teach writing to children at a summer camp and discover that she wants to be a pediatrician who writes a book that helps children understand what's happening to them when they are ill and need to go to the hospital.

Another possibility is for a girl to play out her multiple interests in some kind of sequence. A girl who has what it takes to become a professional basketball star can go to school part-time during her years with a team, and end up with a brand-new career ready to activate when it's time to retire from the court.

Why not explore with your daughter the very exciting concept that she could find a way to make not just one but two or more dreams come true as she heads into the world of tomorrow? That way, in a practical vein, she won't be putting all her eggs in one basket. And even more important, she will be opening herself up to a whole spectrum of life experiences and allowing herself, in the truest sense, to become all she can be.

Activity: I'm Not a One-Note Girl

Have your daughter make a list, with illustrations and captions, of all her interests. Help her by taking pictures of her playing the violin, grooming the dog, cooking, building a tree house, playing softball, reading, doing her science project, and so on.

Resource

Celebrating Girls: Nurturing and Empowering Our Daughters, by Virginia Beane Rutter (Berkeley: Conari Press, 1996).

22

Try It! You Might Like It!

A lot of little girls say they want to be veterinarians, which is not surprising in light of the fact that so many of them have pets. However, as our experience with Take Our Daughters to Work day has shown us, seeing what is really entailed in that career often amazes a girl. An insider's day on the job may make a girl more interested or less interested, depending on how she reacts to the fact that a vet sometimes has to do surgery and that sometimes animals have to be "put to sleep." This is only one example, of course. The point is that when a girl begins at an early age to see close up what actually goes on in a day in the life of a grown woman, she has a chance to assess what the job really entails and make wise choices about her future.

That's why it's a good idea to encourage your daughter to enlist the help of a new mentor next year, even if she got very excited about the work she saw last year. There's a big world out there, and the more jobs you let your daughter know about, the more likely she is to find the one that's right for her. Shop around for willing mentors in a variety of fields and let them take her by the hand into their workplaces and their lives. She may say she's not interested and doesn't want to go, but urge her to give herself the chance to find out firsthand whether any given job could be just the one that would use her abilities to the utmost and make her eager to get up every morning.

April Bethea, a fifteen-year-old from Charlotte, North Carolina, is one girl who wasn't afraid to sample a variety of occupations. "Take Our Daughters to Work day began the year that I was in the fifth grade, and I've participated in the annual event ever since," she writes. "Each year, I look forward to the one day when I'm able to go to work with a professional woman to get an idea of what happens day to day as a working woman." April says she went to work with her mother, an administrative consultant, the first year but that in succeeding years, she branched out. "I've had the chance to work with an executive director of a major arts center in Charlotte, an advertising executive, and a banking officer at First Union Bank," she reports. "All of these in one way or another deal with the communications field and how to be an effective communicator, so it comes as no surprise to myself and others that I'm planning on majoring in journalism/mass communications when I am older."

April's experience is a perfect example of how seeing women in action can help a girl move with her self-esteem intact from the age of ten into the teen years. April also illustrates how seeing a range of jobs can help a girl zero in on the one she wants to pursue. In addition, April displays a heartening faith in her ability to hit the heights: She fully believes she's going to win the Pulitzer Prize one day. And why not? She's certainly got a head start on success and isn't in any way hiding her light under a bushel. She's not measuring her worth by her appearance but by her talents, and she's got ambition to burn.

Take the lesson of April home to your own daughter and make it your business to get her exposed to as many different work environments and job opportunities as possible. She can't dream of being a forensic pathologist if she doesn't even know what that is, and she can't plan to take the prerequisite science and math classes if she doesn't know that's what she needs to do. As April said, "I've spent the day seeing what other women do, not because I don't like going to work with my mom, but because I see the kind of work she does practically every day. Spending the day with other women gives me the opportunity to see what other professional women do in my community."

For that matter, why even stick with your own community? Some girls have written to high-profile women and men and asked for the opportunity to shadow them for a day or even more. Your daughter could have an experience just that thrilling and informative. All it takes is a little nudge from you to get her to try.

Activity: I've Seen and Heard a Lot of Things!

Have your daughter use this section to keep a record of the various work opportunities she has explored. She should devote a page or two to each one, listing her mentor and pasting in photographs of the day. Have her write down her experiences and note the answers she got when she interviewed her mentor. Even more important, have her write down her reactions to the experiences. She should sum up with her feelings about whether she might be interested in pursuing this line of work or whether she isn't sure yet and needs to do more reading and perhaps visit again someday.

Resource

Susan B. Anthony Slept Here: A Guide to American Women's Landmarks, by Lynn Sherr and Jurate Kazickas (New York: Times Books, 1994). This book is another way to expand your daughter's concept of the amazing variety of things women have done and can do. It may also whet her appetite (and yours) to try not only new things but also new places. Travel, as the old chestnut goes, is broadening, and it doesn't have to be expensive. One mother and daughter took a two-week car-and-camping trip across several states, stopping each night at a campground to pitch their tent for a fee of $5 or not much more than that.

23

Let Yourself Grow

"Now you are so tall and turn up your hair, you should remember that you are a young lady," said Meg.

"I'm not! And if turning up my hair makes me one, I'll
wear it in two tails till I'm twenty," cried Jo. "It's bad enough
being a girl anyway when I like boys' games and work. I hate
to think I've got to grow up . . . and sit home and knit, like
a pokey old woman!"

Louisa May Alcott's *Little Women*, 1868

Well over a century has passed since Alcott's beloved young heroines navigated the shoals and eddies of female adolescence. Much
has changed. The telephone, hydroelectricity, the airplane, the radio,
the automobile, computers, and television have been invented, in that
order. There have been two world wars. Minorities and women have
gained the right to vote in this country, and the women's rights movement that began in 1848 has enjoyed a resurgence, starting in the late
1960s and early 1970s. Yet much has not changed. In spite of the fact
that scores of the female members of the baby boom did not "sit home
and knit, like a pokey old woman," but marched into the workplace in
unprecedented numbers, research shows that the majority of little girls
on the threshold of womanhood today are still echoing Jo's lament: "I
hate to think I've got to grow up . . ."

The reasons are complex and legion. We live in a society that can still
be hostile to women and therefore doesn't encourage girls to embrace
womanhood. Add to that the realization that for every individual little
girl, her own passage to adulthood is a journey through uncharted waters. This makes the tenacious problem of low self-esteem in teenage

girls even more understandable. In a sense, every new generation of girls reinvents the wheel when it comes to coping with the radical physical changes that adolescence brings. After all, no matter how many other females have experienced the onset of puberty, when a girl gets her period for the first time, it's front-page news in her own life. Yesterday, she was a coltish, carefree kid, yet overnight she has—unmistakably and with no turning back—become a young woman. There is, of course, a certain pride and awe on the heels of that event, a marveling at the miracle. She is, after all, capable of eventually bringing forth life. But there is a certain terror, too, in this inescapable sign that she is maturing pell-mell, like it or not, and that the magic years of make-believe and make-ready are giving way to Real Life.

What's even more significant, as we have seen, is the uneasy sense that burgeoning womanhood in this society means the loss of the very person a girl once was. Think of Alice, after her dizzying fall down the rabbit hole into a Wonderland where nothing was as it had been. As she said to the Caterpillar: "I know who I was when I got up this morning, but I think I must have changed several times since then. . . . When you have to turn into a chrysalis—you will some day you know—and then after that into a butterfly, I should think you'll feel it a little queer, won't you?"

Obviously, given all of this, one of the most important tasks facing you as the parent of a prepubescent daughter is to let her see the pleasures and realities of growing up. Because women are still made to feel guilty no matter what choices they make—whether to work outside the home or to stay home with children—we need to do a reality check about the signals we send to our daughters. If you're like most American women, you work two shifts—one inside the home and one outside—it's hard not to send your daughter the message that adult life is just one hassle after another. What with juggling job and family, trying to make ends meet, and never having a minute to yourself, you may need to take a very deep breath and reorder your priorities. Yes, for many women, particularly single mothers, the hue and cry about "having it all," which was the slogan of the 1970s and 1980s, has turned into "doing it all." Even so, survey after survey shows that women are proud of all they're accomplishing and while they may be tired, they wouldn't turn the clock back. A 1995 report by the Families and Work Institute, "The New Providers," showed that an amazing nine out of ten women with jobs outside the home would not quit even if they could afford to do so.

What's important, then, is to level with your daughter. Tell her that you do indeed have a lot of responsibilities and that your life sometimes feels like a job for an octopus, but that most of the time you're proud of yourself and pleased with what you do. If you're like a lot of women and you enjoy your work, you may still be somewhat reluctant to talk to your daughter about the pleasures and satisfactions of gainful employment. Give yourself permission to do that. Also, it's important to tell your daughter how good it makes you feel to earn money for yourself and for your family. And show her that you care about and for yourself as well. Make time for your own pursuits and friendships so that she will see that she could do the same if she were in your shoes. In other words, be the kind of role model who lets her know that working and raising a family is a challenge but that the rewards are great—and that sometimes, it's Mom's turn to play.

Beyond that, take yet another opportunity to let your daughter know that if she, like Jo in *Little Women*, enjoys pursuits that have traditionally been labeled "boys' games and work," there is no reason in the world that she can't go right ahead and play those games and do that work, now and in the life she carves out for herself as the years go by.

Activity: I Want to Grow Up!

Have your daughter fold a plain piece of filler paper into eight squares. In each square, she can draw a picture of an activity or responsibility she imagines she might do or have when she grows up. Then she can write a caption for each. She can have some fun with this and picture what the world might be like in the twenty-first century. Will there be space travel? Maybe even space colonies? What will transportation be like? What will the workplace be like? How will she pay bills, manage her money, etc.? What sort of child care will there be? What kinds of sports and games will there be? How will she help other people? Why will they need help? Of course, if she gets really excited about this project, she can use more than one piece of paper!

Resource

Little Women, by Louisa May Alcott. Even if you've read it before, it bears reading again. With an older daughter, take turns reading aloud, or have several girls join in.

24

Color Outside the Lines

Riddle: A father and his daughter are in a car accident and the father is killed. The daughter is rushed to the emergency room, but the doctor on duty says, "I can't treat this girl! She's my daughter!"

Quick, who is the doctor? If you can't guess—or even if you hesitated for a second—you are a victim of the persistent gender stereotyping that still goes on in this society. (The answer, of course, is that the doctor is the girl's mother.) Tell the riddle to your daughter and see whether she can guess the answer. She may not be able to. A lot of girls today can't. Maybe that's because, in spite of decades of progress toward the goal of making women equal partners with the men in their lives and full citizens in this society, women remain a minority in traditionally male professions. Women still hold only 3% of top management positions. That is even more disturbing in light of the fact that women now make up almost half the work force. Also, fewer than 200 women have served in Congress since it began, compared with more than 11,000 men. Major-league sports teams for males have no counterparts for female athletes other than, arguably, basketball players. And there has never been a female vice president of the United States, let alone a president.

We have a long way to go. But if you encourage your daughters to explore nontraditional job opportunities, you can help change the world one girl at a time. Try this exercise with your daughter. Get two pieces of paper and on one of them write WOMEN'S WORK. On the other, write MEN'S WORK. Now, brainstorm lists of occupations traditionally held by women or men. Prime the session by tossing out a few examples and having the children decide which paper to put them on—nurse, plumber, auto mechanic, beautician, secretary, judge. When the girls catch on, let them take the lead. They might come up with truck driver, cook, chef, astronaut, scientist, professor, homemaker, orchestra conductor, editor-in-chief, president, artistic director, stockbroker, kindergarten teacher, construction worker, firefighter, and many more.

> **I'm an actor; I don't understand actress. You don't call doctors doctoresses or doctorettes; you call them doctors.**
> **Whoopi Goldberg**

Be sure you bring up the subject of "gender specific" language here. Do we say "policeman" or "police officer"? "Fireman" or "firefighter"? If we use only language with the gender built right in, the notion gets into our subconscious that only one gender can do that job. This exercise is a real eye-opener and can lead to some healthy laughter when everybody realizes just how close-minded our culture still is. You may want to include your sons in this activity as well, in order to give them a better appreciation of the strictures girls face and to let them think about what rewards traditionally female occupations might hold if boys pursued them.

Once the lists are complete, ask the children to compare women's and men's jobs, looking for patterns such as the number of hours the job entails, the working conditions, the pay, the status, and the authority the job confers on the person. Talk about the skills needed to do the jobs and consider whether any of these skills are gender-based. For example, is there anything about a woman that makes her incapable of running a corporation? Driving a truck? Then share with the children the following excerpt from an essay written by fourteen-year-old Christina Gonzales of Gulfport, Mississippi:

Now my mom, Patricia Lloyd, drives an eighteen-wheeler and has for about ten years. Her route usually goes from California to Florida, but it varies. I have made several trips in the past summers with my mother. I have to have at least ten days to do this. With my mother, I have learned that not everyone has an easy job, but you must do the best you can. My mother is always kind to those she meets on a daily basis even though she has had a hard physical day.

Get the children's reactions to Christina's essay, either orally or in writing. Help them out by asking questions. What would it be like to be away from home for ten days at a time? What kind of "hard physical" labor is Christina referring to? Ask them what they think the pros and cons of being a truck driver might be. Someone might say it would be fun to travel all over the country like that. Someone else might say it would get boring to go back and forth over the same route and eat in restaurants all the time. Now pick another job off your lists, and do the same thing. Have the children try to imagine what the job would be like. Hopefully, this will get them thinking and pique their curiosity so they'll want to learn more about some of the occupations. Have them surf the web to see if they can find information. Visit the library with them. And most important, help your daughter find a way to shadow an adult who does the work in which she has evinced an interest. This would also be a good time to have your son visit a child-care center or go to work with a male nurse. After all, what started as a simple exercise could end up leading to the pursuit of a newfound dream.

<u>**Activity: I Could Do That!**</u>

For this chapter, include the material your daughter gleaned during your research sessions. Have your daughter write a list of traditionally male jobs, using language that doesn't exclude women. Have her write what the job might entail and explain why she could do the job well. If she gets really interested in an occupation or two, have her include copies of letters she writes to potential mentors.

Resource

Mythbusters, Middlesex County VoTech in Perth Amboy, New Jersey; (908) 442-9595. A videotape for young women considering nontraditional careers.

25

Get the Skills You Need to Get Ahead

Amy's mother runs a catering business out of her home, baking holiday specialties and doing weddings, office parties, and bar/bat mitzvahs. From the time Amy was old enough to talk, her mother taught her how to answer the business line. "Kathy's Kitchen. How may I help you?" Amy would chirp confidently. Customers were delighted, and when they said, "May I speak with Kathy, please? I'd like to place an order," Amy would respond with, "Just a moment, please. I'll go get her."

As Amy got older, she learned to write down messages and she learned to cope civilly with the inevitable irate customer. Eventually she learned other office skills, such as preparing invoices and placing ads for the business, and when her mother got a computer, Amy, then nine years old, was the first to learn how to use it. She created a database with fields for the usual client information plus extra ones for things her mother needed to know, such as special dietary restrictions, number of guests, and date of the event. Not surprisingly, Amy also learned to cook like a pro. Overall, her exposure to and participation in her mother's home-based business armed her with myriad tools for success, from the most routine of tasks to the more complex ones such as handling people in an appropriate and courteous manner. Her experience was much like that of children growing up in an earlier era when apprenticeships were common and when youngsters on the farm learned from their parents at an early age. Interestingly, Maria Montessori's highly regarded curriculum for early childhood education is predicated on the premise that very young children want to do real adult work. Unfortunately, most girls today aren't as fortunate as Amy. They are segregated from the world of work and have no clear idea of what their parents do all day that makes them so weary when they get home in the evening.

If your daughter has few chances to be around you and other adults in the workplace, you can make up for this by encouraging her to start and run a business of her own. Baby-sitting is an obvious possibility, but even if that's what she decides to do, discuss with her ways to make her services more professional. She could design a business card for herself on the computer, or order some from a catalogue. She could print flyers, possibly giving her business a name. She could collect references. She could write a résumé. She could use a database or a notebook to keep track of her clients, noting the birth dates of the children and any special needs, as well as other information about the household, such as pets, parents' rules about TV and computer use, bedtime, and emergency numbers. And she could keep track of her earnings, savings, and spending. All of these activities will be getting her used to behaving in an organized, businesslike manner and will stand her in good stead in the years to come.

Beyond baby-sitting, think about other possibilities. One thirteen-year-old had a talent for woodcarving that she discovered in shop class. She made a walking stick with an intricate design for her grandfather's birthday, and he was so impressed that he suggested she ought to go commercial. She made several items—another walking stick, a jewelry box, a plaque that read "Number 1 Mom"—and then showed them to the director of the community youth center. The director agreed that the girl could use a corner of the lobby to sell her wares and take orders. She painted a professional-looking sign and set up a card table, and she was in business. Her items sold faster than she could turn them out, and before long she had made a killing. All the while, she was learning invaluable skills that would soon become second nature to her and help her get ahead in the future. She was keeping track of expenses and time spent, making sure her products were cost-effective, setting her prices accordingly, organizing her life so that she could fulfill orders in a timely fashion, correcting problems if certain designs didn't work, and doing all the paperwork on the family computer. (Needless to say, with all that money jingling in her pocket and all those people using the items she had created, she was also feeling pretty good about herself.)

Think about your daughter's talents and interests and see what she could do. Maybe she could write a neighborhood newsletter or cut lawns or deliver the paper or walk dogs or take care of pets while people are away or build birdhouses. Whatever she does, she'll be learning a lot and gaining a full measure of pride in her accomplishments.

Activity: It's My Own Business

Have your daughter use this section of her book to keep copies of her résumé, flyers, business cards, and invoices and to keep track of expenses and earnings.

Resources

An Income of Her Own, 1804 West Burbank Blvd., Burbank, CA 91506; 800-350-2978; (web site) http://www.AnIncomeofHerOwn.com

The Entrepreneurial Development Institute, 2025 I Street, NW, Suite 115, Washington, D.C. 20006; 202-822-8334; (web site) http://www.bedrock.com.tedi/tedi.htm

26

You're Not "Daddy's Little Girl"

At a fire station in Aurora, Colorado, the guys used to bring their sons in all the time to see what was going on. They let them slide down the pole and help polish up the bright red trucks and try on the helmets. Sometimes when things were quiet, a boy would get to sit in the driver's seat and make vr-o-o-o-m, vr-o-o-o-m noises while he pretended to steer. And every now and then when a call would come in, a lucky little boy who happened to be there would get to ride on the truck with his dad as it sped along, sirens blaring, on the way to an heroic mission. The sons were all very proud of their brave fathers, and a lot of them wanted to grow up to fight fires just the way their dads did.

Then one of the men heard about Take Our Daughters to Work day. It was as if a cartoon lightbulb had lit up over his head. Why hadn't he ever brought his *daughter* to the station? he suddenly wondered. Why hadn't he let *her* sit in the driver's seat and feel the adrenaline rush of doing something as meaningful as saving people's lives? He mentioned this to the other guys, and they all saw his point. And so on a sun-splashed April afternoon, a group of very eager and very excited little girls got a taste of what it could be like to grow up to be as courageous and important as their fathers were.

Take Our Daughters to Work day has helped many fathers open their minds to the possibility that daughters can drive fire trucks and run corporations and run for office and conduct scientific research and play basketball and be stockbrokers and do countless other things once thought to be male-only preserves. When we started Take Our Daughters to Work day, we got thousands of enthusiastic and concerned letters from people who cared about girls and who saw that something was going wrong at adolescence for the girls they loved. They wanted to intervene. A large percentage of those letters were from the girls' fathers.

A supportive father—who makes a girl feel good about the fact that she's smart and capable and curious and somebody very special in her own right—gives his daughter the green light to go where she wants to go in life. In fact, a study from the University of Michigan found that fathers were particularly important as a source of encouragement for women going into science, math, and engineering. As a father, think hard about whether you are providing that kind of encouragement for your daughter. Especially as she emerges in adolescence and begins to look womanly, guard against comments about her appearance that might reinforce society's message that her looks are what is most valued. Treat her with respect and teach your sons to do the same. Also, watch TV with her and let her know that you don't buy into the limited images of women that are so often shown. And contradict "lookism." If both your daughter and your son have dressed neatly for a trip to grandmother's house, you might say, "Hey, you guys look great!" But avoid singling out your daughter. And above all, remember that girls learn that they deserve respect from men when they see their fathers treat the women in their lives—family, friends, and co-workers—with respect. If a girl lives in a home where her mother has respect and power, her love for her father will take on a whole different meaning.

On a more practical level, teach your daughter to cast a line, catch a ball, hammer a nail, play chess. There is nothing gender-based about any of those activities. And when she catches her first fish, fields a fly ball, builds a tree house, or cries out "Checkmate!" you'll have a daughter whose self-esteem is swelling and who will be determined to carry with her into adult life the feeling of accomplishment and the heady taste of victory you will have instilled in her. She'll also know that batting her eyelashes and being coy is not the way to have a genuine bond and a real relationship with a man. You are, after all, the first man she ever loved. Make sure she gets all the right messages. Specifically, be on the lookout for any attempts to jump in and "rescue" your daughter if she's struggling with a situation in which you would expect a son to stick it out or solve the problem himself.

Activity: I'm More Than Daddy's Little Girl

Father and daughter can write an essay together about all the things they enjoy and about their experiences watching TV with a critical eye. They can also draw pictures or paste in photographs of themselves together, fishing or playing chess or fixing the car or cleaning up the yard. If your daughter does not have a father or if her father is essentially absentee, see whether you can find a male role model for her—an uncle, a neighbor, a grandfather—who can give her a positive experience about relationships between males and females. If so, then ask the man who is like a father to her to participate in this chapter of her book.

Resources

How to Father a Successful Daughter, by Nicky Marone (New York: Ballantine, 1988).

Working Father: New Strategies for Balancing Work and Family, by James A. Levine and Todd Pittinsky (Reading, MA: Addison-Wesley, 1997).

27

Girls Need a Good Education

When Casey Fitzmaurice, a sixteen-year-old from Hingham, Mass-achusetts, went to work with her father, a human resources man-ager, she was struck by the connection between education and success. "I got to sit in on an interview my father had scheduled that day. The résumés my father sees reflect a lifetime of a student's work, which made me realize that my future depends on my getting as much out of school as I can. I started high school this year, and I now see that many of the things I'm doing right now affect the way the rest of my life un-folds."

Casey is right, and yet statistics about girls' performance in school in this country are alarming. The following was reported in *Daughters*, a newsletter for parents of girls ages eight to eighteen, which you can visit at http://www.daughters.org (or call 800-829-1088):

- In the early grades, girls are ahead of or equal to boys on almost every standardized measure of achievement and psychological well-being. By the time they graduate from high school or college, they have fallen back.

- In high school, girls score lower on the SAT and ACT tests, which are critical for college admission. The greatest gender gap is in the crucial areas of science and math.
- Girls score far lower on College Board Achievement tests, which are required by most highly selective colleges.
- Boys are more likely to be awarded state and national college scholarships.
- The gap does not narrow in college. Women score lower on all sections of the Graduate Record Exam, which is necessary to enter many graduate programs.

In other words, girls enter school ahead of boys but leave behind them. Girls are as smart as boys are. In certain ways, they are even smarter. So what happens along the way? A 1992 study done by the American Association of University Women, "How Schools Short-change Girls," documented the way teachers treat boys and girls differently. In classrooms, boys are twice as likely to be seen as role models. Boys are five times as likely to get teachers' attention and twelve times as likely to be heard in class. In textbooks, one-seventh of all illustrations of children are girls. Teachers choose more classroom activities that appeal to boys than to girls. Pupils are exposed to almost three times as many stories with boys as heroes as stories with girls as heroes. Boys are more often portrayed as clever, courageous, creative, and resourceful, while girls are shown to be compassionate, dependent, and docile.

Share this information with your daughter and find out whether she sees herself and her school experience in the research. One mother reports that her fifth-grade daughter said this: "The boys are always talking and acting stupid, so the teacher is always going, like, 'Jason, zip your mouth' and 'David, keep your hands to yourself.' Then if the boys sit still and pay attention for like five minutes, she gets all excited and tells them how proud she is. If boys do anything right, people make a fuss about it." There is no question that boys demand an unfair share of teachers' attention. Short of sending your daughter to a single-sex school—and the National Coalition of Girls' Schools would recommend doing just that—is there any way you can make sure she succeeds in school? Start by emphasizing the importance of education. Some families make up an assigned reading list and give oral reports to one another, followed by discussions. Also, whenever your daughter goes to a worksite, whether on Take Our Daughters to Work day or on other days you plan for her, remind her to ask questions about what kind of education is necessary for the jobs she sees. And whenever there is a gathering of friends and family at your house, steer the conversation around to the value of education.

Beyond that, David Sadker, coauthor with the late Myra Sadker of *Failing at Fairness: How Our Schools Cheat Girls* and the father of two girls, recommends getting involved in your daughter's homework, showing her that what she's doing in school is extremely important to you and to her future. Have her read her essays aloud to you. Talk about what she's written and validate her opinions. Also, Sadker suggests visiting the classroom and observing whether attention and praise are given more liberally to boys than to girls.

Above all, remember that girls watch and listen to what is important to the adults in their lives. Education can be a lifelong pursuit, and if you are taking courses or learning new skills through reading, that sets a very good example for your daughter. Naturally, you'll benefit as well!

For further information, you can order a catalog of excellent gender-equity materials from the Women's Education Equity Act (WEEA) Resource Center, Education Development Center, Inc. Phone: 800-225-3088 or 800-793-5076. Another source: *The Equity News-letter*, from the Marymount Institute for the Education of Women and Girls, Marymount Avenue, Tarrytown, NY 10591-3796, 914-332-4917.

And finally, encourage your daughter to stay in school. In the next century, only 14% of all jobs will be available to workers with less than a high-school education.

Activity: I'm a Good Student

Have her keep a record of her study habits and copies of her report cards, plus any special awards or certificates she earns.

Resource

SchoolGirls: Young Women, Self-Esteem, and the Confidence Gap, by Peggy Orenstein (New York: Doubleday, 1994).

28

Math and Science Are Not Guy Things

Once upon a time, there was a twelve-year-old girl who wanted to be a fashion designer. She was a gifted artist and she spent a lot of time drawing pictures of fluttery dresses and jazzed-up jeans and wedding gowns and skating costumes. Even when she was a very little girl, she had made clothes for her dolls, cutting out circles of fabric with a hole for the neck and a length of ribbon for the belt. She used to tell her mother that she hated school, especially math, and that she wished she could just quit school and draw fashion designs all day. Then she and her mother heard about Take Our Daughters to Work day. With a little effort, they found a fashion designer the girl could shadow. The girl was really excited, and she prepared a list of questions to ask her mentor. Imagine her surprise when the fashion designer had this to say: "One of the most important things you need to do is study math and computer skills. We have to calculate exactly how a garment will fit the body. Designing clothes requires a lot more than drawing. It's a very scientific process."

Maybe boys are inherently better at math and maybe not, and maybe girls are socialized to have math anxiety, but whatever the case, it's a moot point. Girls who want to have challenging and rewarding careers in just about any field that can be imagined need to know they must take the math courses and earn the grades they need to get ahead. Math is not for boys only, even if it seems to come more easily for most of them. If your daughter whines that math is too hard or too boring or if she says she's not good at it, the response needs to be "How can I help?" Then tell her to stop wasting time and get cracking on that math homework.

In *Reviving Ophelia*, Mary Pipher writes: "Girls need to be encouraged to persevere in spite of difficulty, to calm down and believe in themselves. They need permission to take their time and to make many mistakes before solving the problem. They need to learn relaxation skills to deal with the math anxiety so many experience."

One of the most successful efforts in schools has been to invite women engineers and scientists into the classrooms to talk to girls about their work and history with math and science. Consider initiating a program like this in your daughter's school. Also, letting your daughter know that you believe in her ability to succeed in math and science will strengthen her resolve. One mother, herself a math professor, tells the story of how her daughter was placed in a low-level section for math in grade school even though she had been weaned on math games and activities. The mother

> **I** was taught that the way of progress is neither swift nor easy.
>
> **Marie Curie**

and daughter went together to speak to the daughter's teacher. The mother told him she was positive her daughter could handle the more advanced work, and the teacher agreed to let her try. The daughter was so heartened by her mother's faith in her that she applied herself with determination and asked for help when she needed it. She did herself and her mother proud—and is now in college, majoring in mathematics.

To help your daughter in math, and in science as well, look into fun, successful after-school programs such as:

- Operation SMART™, offered through Girls Incorporated. Contact Girls, Inc., at 212-689-3700, or visit them at http:// www. girlsinc.org.

- Family Math, part of Project EQUALS, provides opportunities for parents and children to do hands-on math under the direction of teachers or community leaders. For information, write or call Lawrence Hall of Science, University of California, Berkeley, CA 94705; 510-642-1823.

Activity: I Don't Want to Shortchange Myself

Have your daughter interview girls not much older than she is—seniors in high school and freshmen in college—as well as young women just starting out in a variety of careers. Your daughter's goal is to find out which math and science courses the girls still in school are taking in preparation for their work, and to find out from the young women working outside the home whether or not they are using math and science on the job. (One girl who did this couldn't find a single woman who wasn't using math, and most of her interviewees were using science as well.)

Resource

Women and Numbers: Lives of Women Mathematicians, by Teri Perl (San Carlo, CA: Wide World Publishing/Tetra, 1993). Stories about the lives of female mathematicians plus related math activities.

Science Is Women's Work: Photos and Biographies of American Women in the Sciences, by Nancy Gallop (Windsor, CA: National Women's History Project, 1993).

29

Get Wired!

Technology jobs are destined to be the most lucrative ones of the next century, and girls need to be ready to compete for those jobs. To that end, on a brisk and burnished November Saturday in 1997, hundreds of girls between the ages of nine and thirteen came to the De Vry Institute of Technology in New Brunswick, New Jersey, where they deftly rewired telephones, took apart and reassembled computers, and logged onto the Internet. They did all of this under the tutelage of an eager cadre of college-age female mentors. The occasion was the first ever TechGRRRLS Day, a kickoff for the YWCA's TechGRRRLS! Clubs, a program designed to raise girls' interest and competence in the crucial area of technology, while helping them to develop their critical thinking and problem-solving skills. "It is vital that we encourage girls at an early age," said Prema Mathai-Davis, CEO of the YWCA of the U.S.A. "This program gives girls a network of supportive role models to help them see and achieve their goals."

This is a huge and refreshing change from the days—not so long ago—when the typical woman was in the habit of wringing her hands helplessly and saying she couldn't program the VCR, or unpacking the new stereo but waiting until her husband got home so he could hook it up. Females can't afford to be technophobes anymore, and giving girls the idea that they are not "mechanically minded" is risky business these days.

Relate all of this to your daughter's life, even if you can't afford a computer for her. You can call organizations such as the YWCA or Girls, Inc., to see whether there are programs or clubs she could participate in. Also, if you have shied away from the Internet thus far, jump in for your sake as well as for your daughter's. It's really not difficult at all. And as with any new skill, the more you and your daughter work at finding your way around, the easier your cybertravels will become.

You might also want to create your own website. The big Internet service providers offer help in doing so. If you do get a computer for your home, however, be sure you also have parental control software such as Net Nanny or Cybersitter. You want to be sure that your daughter's travels on the web are safe. In addition, think about purchasing software that schedules the time each family member spends on the Internet.

Activity: I'm a Tech Girl!

If you have a home computer and your daughter creates a web page, have her print it out and put it in her book. If she joins a local computer club for girls, have her bring home printouts for her book. She can also write about or paste in e-mail from a pen pal—maybe a girl her age in Australia or Germany who is also a "tech girl." In addition, anything she creates on the computer—a flyer or business cards for her business, a form letter she personalizes for various potential mentors, invoices, mailing labels, schedules, calendars, digitized photos, etc.—can be a part of this chapter of her book.

Resource

The Neuter Computer: Computers for Girls and Boys, by Jo Sanders and Antonia Stone (New York: Neal-Schuman Publishers, 1986).

30

Take the First Step

One of the stories that inspired us to create Take Our Daughters to Work day involved a girl whose high-school counselor sent her on an interview for an internship at a company in Manhattan. The girl traveled to the building where the company was headquartered, but she just couldn't go through the door. She'd never been to a skyscraper like that before, and she was overwhelmed. She turned and went back home. Her counselor made a second appointment. Again, the girl traveled to the building, and this time she worked up her nerve to go through the door. But standing on the marble floor of the massive lobby, she froze. She never made it to the elevator bank. Once again, she went back home.

Fortunately, her counselor and the person she was to have seen were on her side. A third appointment was scheduled. The counselor told the girl she believed in her and knew she could find the courage to go to the interview. The counselor told her to think of her task as a series of steps, two of which she had already managed to take: arriving at the building and going through the door. Now all she needed was to take those two steps again and add the third one: taking the elevator to the office where she was to have her interview. The counselor said she knew the girl would succeed. And she did. On her third try, she went thought the revolving doors, walked across that marble lobby, rode the elevator to the fortieth floor, stepped out into the carpeted reception area, and stated her business. The interview went very well, and the girl got the internship—an opportunity that would turn out to be the start of a bright new chapter in her life.

Barbara Sher, best-selling author of *Live the Life You Love: In Ten Easy Step-by-Step Lessons*, says the key is to take the first step, however small it may be. Does your daughter talk about wanting to be a playwright? Go to the library with her and get a book that shows the standard manuscript format for writing plays. If you have a computer, get one of the software packages for playwrights. If you don't have a computer, look into renting one or ask her teacher if she could use the school computer after hours. Or help your daughter start a savings account earmarked for buying a computer. Give her a little venture capital as a start and encourage her to squirrel away some of her allowance each week toward this purchase. The idea is to do at least one tangible thing that gets her going toward her goal.

> **D**on't wait for your "ship to come in," and feel angry and cheated when it doesn't. Get going with something small.
>
> **Irene Kassorla**

After that, Sher suggests breaking the journey into little, manageable steps—just as the girl who was at first afraid to go into the building for her interview finally did—so that your daughter won't be daunted by the enormity of the task and lose her energy and drive. Check some plays out of the library for her to read. Take her to plays if possible, even school productions if that's all that's available. Look into camps that have creative writing programs. And encourage her to write to someone she admires—say, Wendy Wasserstein or Anna Deveare Smith—for advice. Explain to her that she can write to the playwright in care of the publisher of the plays she's read. And encourage her to try her hand at a little writing every single day.

The same process works for any dream. The beauty of this is that by taking the first step, and then a few more steps, your daughter will find out whether she is really interested in the dream or not. Maybe she thought she wanted to be a dentist, but when she took the first step and shadowed a dentist for a day, she found that she hated being around people in pain. Or, just the opposite, perhaps she found that she absolutely loved the idea of being skilled at helping people in pain. Whatever the outcome, taking the first step gets her out of the realm of aimless daydreaming and into the real world of making progress toward becoming a woman of accomplishment.

Remember, as an anonymous pundit once put it, a journey of a thousand miles begins with a single step. Beyond that, remember that one step leads to another. When you take a first step, the second step doesn't seem so difficult. When you take the second step, the third one seems a lot easier—and before you know it, you're off and running! Actually, this is a principle your daughter can use in every aspect of her life. A term paper might seem like a huge, overwhelming project, but if she writes down the steps she'll need to take—go to the library, go to the computer room at school, interview someone, write an outline, etc.— she'll reduce the task into small, possible steps. Then if she writes a schedule for herself and sticks to it day by day, she'll get the job done and won't waste any time worrying and procrastinating. Also, Barbara Sher suggests giving oneself a little reward at various points along the way. With the term paper example, for your daughter might tell herself that when she gets to the outline stage and can cross that off her list, she can afford to take a day away from the project and do something fun like biking in the state park or treating herself to a new CD she's been saving up for. Then the next day, she'll get back to work with renewed vigor and resolve. What she's learning here is a strategy for perseverance—an important life lesson if there ever was one!

Activity: I Took the First Step

This chapter in your daughter's book can have two components. One is a plan she makes for accomplishing a goal that's important to her— getting top marks in the state music competition, improving her math grade, making the soccer team, memorizing lines for the school play. The other is a list of rewards. Help her think of something besides candy or a TV show. Even offer to do something special with her, such as going to a movie, or let her have a sleepover. Be careful not to take her shopping, however, or buy her expensive gifts. You don't want her to equate spending money with doing a good job. The rewards she gets should have some value in and of themselves—recreation, exercise, friendship, music.

Resource

I Could Do Anything If I Only Knew What It Was, by Barbara Sher (New York: Delacorte Press, 1994).

Live the Life You Love: In Ten Easy Step-by-Step Lessons, by Barbara Sher (New York: Dell Publishing, 1996).

31

Be Prepared

We've worked with many concerned parents who realized too late that leaving career preparation entirely up to their daughters' schools was not always a wise move. As advances in technology change more job descriptions every year, parents need to stay informed, involved, and active in their daughters' planning for future jobs.

For example, if your daughter wants to be a writer, it's not enough for her to scribble in her journal. It's not even enough for her to read, read, read—although that's a good idea. What she needs if she's going to succeed in the publishing world of the twenty-first century is to learn Quark and HTML. Does she realize that? Why not have her talk with someone in the industry today in order to get an idea of just what she has to do now to prepare for the future? Also, look at the want ads with her. A recent one in *The New York Times* under the heading of "editorial" reads like this:

Research, reporting, editing and production of event guides, articles, links, multimedia interactive features, forums and special projects. Requirements: solid computer skills, interactive media experience, knowledge of HTML, attention to detail, ability to meet deadlines in a daily production environment; Photoshop, Quark and other applications experience a plus. We offer competitive salaries commensurate with experience, a comprehensive benefits package and the opportunity to go as far as your talents will take you in a stimulating entrepreneurial environment.

Of course, people still write books and magazine pieces and newspaper articles, but even if your daughter aspires to be a novelist or a columnist or a foreign correspondent, she would do well to be electronically literate. One writer we know who sold her first story back in 1967 has this to say: "Years ago, I wrote my drafts in longhand. I rewrote by literally cutting and pasting. Then I'd pay someone to type the pages for me because I had never learned to touch-type. I wanted to take chorus in high school and it conflicted with the typing class! But if a girl were to ask me now what she needs to do to become a writer, I couldn't emphasize enough that she absolutely has to type like the wind and know how to use a computer and be conversant with the Internet. Otherwise, she'll be left in the dust."

This writer managed to catch up from behind by learning to type and getting computer skills, "so I wouldn't be a dinosaur." She even writes a monthly column on an "e-zine" on the web and sends her HTML documents to the publisher via e-mail. But your daughter can get a head start on success if she plans to take the right courses right now in junior high and high school in order to be prepared for college and eventually for the workplace. The writer who needs to be computer-literate is just one example. Beyond technology, there are many things a girl needs to learn to be prepared. Help your daughter research the prerequisites for her chosen career and help her find mentors in that field to tell her what they wish they had known when they were her age.

> **I**'m not afraid of storms, for I'm learning how to sail my ship.
>
> **Louisa May Alcott**

This is also another area in which finding young mentors is a wonderful idea. Girls just a few years older than she is and young women perhaps ten years older than she is can give her the wisdom of hindsight (I wish I had taken calculus—I wish I hadn't been such a goof-off senior year) and, in a more positive vein, give her the sense that she could reach their level of success and competence. Sometimes the life experiences of an adult mentor are more than a very young girl can absorb, but a girl or young woman closer to her own age presents an attainable role model.

Also, if your daughter is still in grade school, arrange for her to talk to a junior-high guidance counselor now. And if she is in junior high, get her in touch with a senior-high counselor. Have her begin to map out what courses she needs and when she can take them in order to fit everything in.

Activity: I'm Going to Get Ready!

Have your daughter map out the big picture—which courses she'll take in school and what plans she might have for college and beyond. She can make several different plans if she wants to.

Resource

I Can Be What I Want to Be, a planning workbook for junior high students and their parents developed by the National Black Child Development Institute and Women's Educational Equity Act Program, United States Department of Education, printed and distributed by the National Black Child Development Institute, 1463 Rhode Island Ave., NW, Washington, D.C., 20005.

32

Choose Your Own Adventure

S ome years ago, there was a popular series of children's books in which there were several endings to the mystery or the quest the young hero and heroine were engaged in. The reader, at a certain point in the text, had the power to make a decision that would alter the course of the story and send him or her off toward one of the endings. Of course, it was possible to start again from the beginning and make a different decision and see what outcome that choice would lead to. For a girl with her whole life ahead of her, thinking about and planning for the future is a lot like those choose-your-own-adventure books. She is, after all, the author of the story of her life. True, there are things over which she has no control, such as how many brothers and sisters she has or how tall she will grow or whether or not her parents get divorced or where she lives as a child. But when it comes to deciding what to make of her talents and abilities and passions as she grows up, she's the one who calls the shots. That's a very powerful concept.

Try this exercise with your daughter. Tell her to imagine that she has lived to be in her eighties. Ask her to look back on her long life and write a biographical sketch. Help her out by posing the following questions, either on the computer or on index cards:

- Where have you lived? Describe the place or places.
- What kinds of work have you done and what was its purpose?
- Were you famous or did you make an impact in your own quiet way?
- Did you say anything that might go down in history?
- Did you make any changes in your community or in the world?
- If so, how did you do that?
- Did you have a family? If so, describe the family.
- Did you have favorite leisure activities? If so, describe them.
- Did you travel? If so, where did you go?

If she's stumped—for example, if she writes that she lived in Alaska but can't describe it—help her out by pointing her to some sources like the encyclopedia or a site on the web or a book about Alaska. The same goes for other questions. Help her research jobs, leisure activities, and travel destinations. She can write this "adventure" many

All adventures, especially into new territory, are scary.

Sally Ride

times over, imagining herself in different locales, doing different jobs, making her mark in different ways, and enjoying life in different ways. All along, she'll be soaking up information and opening up her mind to a world of possibilities for choosing the real-life adventure that would be the most wonderful of all.

Now have your daughter interview female relatives—aunts, grandmothers, great-grandmothers—about the adventures that are their lives. She will not only gain insights and ideas, but she'll realize that she is part of a family chain of admirable women who love her and are her biggest boosters.

Activity: I'm a Girl with a Great Future

The stories she has written about her future go into this chapter. She can illustrate them if she likes.

Resource

Girls to the Rescue, a three-volume set edited by Bruce Lansky (Minnetonka, MN: Meadowbrook Press, 1995). These are tales of clever, courageous girls from around the world. They feature adventurous girl heroines with enough drive and imagination to save the day.

Part Three

Command Respect

33

Your Opinions Count

One year on Take Our Daughters to Work day, several fathers who were high-level employees for a major health insurance company brought their girls, ages nine to thirteen, along. The first order of the morning was a meeting of the top brass to discuss investment opportunities for the corporation, and the girls took seats at the big, oval conference table. Several fathers whispered to their daughters that the things to be discussed would probably be boring but that they wanted their daughters to be good girls and sit quietly. As soon as the CEO arrived and some papers were passed around, the discussion began. Not long into it, the subject of investing in a tobacco company was brought up. The idea was greeted with enthusiasm all around. The tobacco company's stock had been performing beautifully, and there was very shortly a consensus that the tobacco stock should be added to the insurance company's portfolio.

The CEO moved on to the next topic, but the girls around the table glanced at one another. They didn't say anything at the time, but on a break they talked about the decision with one another in the rest room. They all agreed that they thought the decision was wrong. Then during lunch, one of the girls said to her father, "We learned in school that cigarettes kill people. Why do you want to put money in a company that makes something that kills people?" The father of the little girl looked at her with new eyes, and said, "You are a very smart person. I hope you'll always say what you think is right, the way you just did." And the father promised to speak to the CEO about changing the decision.

A year later, on Take Our Daughters to Work day, this father brought his daughter with him again, as did many other parents of the girls who had been at the original meeting. This time, there was a special breakfast for the girls and their parents and mentors. The CEO stood up, cleared his throat, and said: "We would like to welcome our daughters once again. Some of the girls I see here were with us last year and participated in a meeting that resulted in our company investing in tobacco stock. I was informed that the girls felt this decision was a mistake. I am happy to announce that as of last week, this company has divested itself of all tobacco stock. We appreciate the fact that our daughters had the courage to speak up and teach us a lesson. Thank you, girls. We value your opinions, and look forward to your input today and in the years to come."

The girl who spoke to her father about the tobacco stock is now in her teens, and she has carried with her into adolescence the memory of how she refused to "be a good girl," but rather opened her mouth to speak out against something she believed was wrong. She has also remembered the fact that affirming her opinion with other girls helped her clarify her beliefs and ultimately make a change for the better.

Girls and women can change the world for the better as long as they don't let their voices be silenced and their opinions be ignored. Taking action and speaking out for just causes are the keys to girls growing up healthy and strong. One safe way to begin when your daughter is young is to include her insofar as possible in family decisions such as what to name a new pet, where to go on an outing, what movie to see, which video to rent. Get into the habit of brainstorming—a technique that involves people tossing out ideas for whatever they're worth, with the assurance that no one else will shoot them down or ridicule them. For example, if you have just brought home a kitten from the shelter, sit down together and bandy about some ideas about what to name the newcomer. If your daughter offers a suggestion that her brother doesn't like, he is simply not allowed to say, "That's stupid!" Then when you have lots of suggestions, take a vote. Whether or not one of your daughter's suggestions wins isn't the point. What matters is that she knows that her suggestions are worthy and that they count for something. Maybe next time, one of her suggestions will be the winner.

On a larger scale, you and your daughter can work together to draft petitions for things you feel need changing—maybe the fact that there are not enough biographies of famous women in the school library or not enough opportunities for girls to participate in sports. You and your daughter can also write letters to your mayor, governor, and congressional representatives asking for changes you feel are necessary. And you can also write letters to editors of magazines and newspapers. Imagine the sense of power and self-respect your daughter will feel if even a few of her efforts turn out to make a difference. TV personality Linda Ellerbee tells the story of a young girl who wrote to a company that makes dishwashers, pointing out that their ads showed only women loading and unloading their product. The ads were changed as a result to include men.

Still on the subject of writing her opinions, your daughter may want to contribute to a magazine called *blue jean*, which publishes the work of girls and young women. And whether or not she contributes, she will be empowered by reading the work of her peers. Call 888-4BLU-JEAN to order a subscription. There is also another biannual magazine written by girls and young women called *HUES* (Hear Us Emerging Sisters), which features political writing. The number is 800-HUES-4U2. *Teen Voices* is another excellent choice. Call 888-882-TEEN.

Another excellent way to give your daughter practice in speaking her mind is to form a book club. *The Mother-Daughter Book Club*, by Shireen Dodson is both a novel and a manual about how to start a club.

To get you started, here are some books that feature strong heroines who are good examples of girls who know their opinions count:

The Witch of Blackbird Pond, by Elizabeth George Speare.

Catherine Called Birdy, by Karen Cushman.

Activity: I'm a Girl Who Counts (and Counts Girls)

This chapter of your daughter's book is a research project, and you can share it with her. Help her find statistics about the number of women in a variety of professions, and the number of women in high-level positions. In other words, literally count the women who count in any given occupation. Have her write or draw her reaction to what she learns from this and ask her if she can think of ways that she, together with other girls, might act at the local level to change those numbers for the better.

Resource

Great Books for Girls, by Kathleen Odean (New York: Ballantine Books, 1997). A listing of more than 600 books to inspire today's girls and tomorrow's women.

34

Don't Let Anybody Else Do the Talking for You

Certainly, it is frustrating and bewildering when a formerly outspoken daughter clams up during prepubescence. But you're not doing a girl a favor if you speak for her.

A sixth-grade teacher in a New York City public school says she's constantly amazed at how a lot of parents can't control the urge to speak for their children—particularly their daughters, who are often more reticent at eleven than the boys. "I had a mother bring a new student to meet me when the family moved here about two months into the school year," the teacher says. "The girl was tall for her age and already maturing, and she was just standing there looking at her shoes. I didn't force anything, but I spoke directly to her in a friendly manner, starting with the usual questions, like 'What's your name?' and 'Where did you live before you moved here?' The kid would hesitate and the mother would jump right in as if her daughter were mute. Then the mother started talking *about* her daughter as though she weren't even in the room. The mother went on and on saying, 'Oh, she's very shy. I'm really sorry. She just isn't very talkative. She's big for her age, and I think that embarrasses her. I thought you ought to know she's kind of clumsy when it comes to gym class. She'll probably grow out of it, but right now, she's got two left feet and she can't catch a ball to save her life. Of course, it doesn't help that she's nearsighted. She doesn't get any peripheral vision with her glasses. We'll get her contacts when she's thirteen, but for now she's at a disadvantage. And then there's the problem with her handwriting. See, she has always had trouble with her descenders, and her teacher last year told us . . .'

"Of course, this mother meant well. She was trying to apologize for her daughter's shyness and protect her from problems in the new school, but all she did was mortify the girl and prevent her from ever getting up the nerve to look at the teacher, let alone say anything to her."

Rather than speak for your daughter, what you want to do is to give her a chance to form what she wants to say and to be her own spokesperson. Even if you are praising your daughter, you're still depriving her of a chance to authorize herself if you say what she could say herself. One mother, intensely proud of her sixteen-year-old daughter's accomplishments, was excited about introducing the girl to a business colleague for the first time. During dinner, the colleague would speak to the girl, saying something such as, "I understand you're directing the school play. That is fascinating." Then the girl would open her mouth but before she could get a word out, the mother would say, "Oh, yes, it's the first time they've ever let a student do the directing! I went to a rehearsal the other day, and you should have seen the way Carla was handling everything. She had rehearsal schedules all printed out, she had the blocking all set, she was dealing with all these different personalities, dealing with the actors who weren't off-book when they should have been. It was amazing!"

> **R**esponsibility to yourself means refusing to let others do your thinking, talking, and naming for you.
>
> **Adrienne Rich**

On the way home from dinner, the mother told Carla she was so glad the colleague had gotten to know her. "Mom," Carla said, "she didn't get to know me at all! You were just *telling* her about me. I might as well not even have been there. You could have had the same conversation if I had been in *Australia.*"

So, mothers and fathers alike, be watchful of speaking for your daughters. Get out of the habit of being your daughter's mouthpiece.

That way, as Carol Gilligan puts it, you'll get a chance to hear what she *really* thinks instead of what you think she thinks—or worse, what she thinks you *want* her to think. Even more important, by giving her the airtime she needs and deserves, you'll be reaffirming her value as an individual and ingraining in her the knowledge that as she continues to grow and to get out into the world on her own, she can be a person in her own right. In *Mother Daughter Revolution*, DeBold, Wilson, and Malavé write about giving your daughter "voice lessons." They contend that as adult women, we know that there is sometimes a price to pay for speaking our minds, and we rush in to protect our daughters. But what we need to do is step back and let our daughters raise their voices so that a new generation of women will truly be seen and heard.

> **O**ne of the things about equality is not just that you be treated equally to a man, but that you treat yourself equally to the way you treat a man.
>
> **Marlo Thomas**

Activity: I'm a Girl Who Wants to Speak for Herself

Have your daughter write her recollections of times when someone else jumped in and spoke for her. Have her write what she would have said if she could have. Ask her if she will share the results with you, and promise you'll keep your sense of humor if you see yourself in what she has written. Talk about how you could behave differently in the future.

Resource

Girl Power: Young Women Speak Out, by Hillary Carlip (New York: Warner Books, 1995).

35

Don't Sell Yourself Short

Women have historically been cast in the role of helpmate, the "woman behind the man." Some women in that role—Eleanor Roosevelt, for example—were visible members of society. As she once said, "No one can make you feel inferior without your consent." However, for many women, the roles of wife and mother meant staying behind the scenes and achieving by helping husbands and offspring achieve. That was certainly a valuable contribution, and yet many of those women were not recognized as having accomplished anything in their own right. In fact, back then, a woman who thought highly of herself was considered vain, and a girl who had an elevated opinion of herself was told she was too big for her britches. Women and girls were expected to be modest and docile, to stay out of the limelight and never, ever to brag or swagger the way a boy or a man would. That was simply not ladylike.

Times have changed. Girls need to know how to "brag and swagger." In the real world, your daughter will need to be able to do that or she'll risk missing out on opportunities. She'll also, on a more practical level, risk being passed over for promotions and raises. Men are still ahead of women when it comes to knowing how to sell themselves, and women need to acquire that skill. While you're helping your daughter do that, why not look deep inside yourself to see whether there is a part of you that feels it's somehow "not right" for a female to sing her own praises? Many, many women across the country have told us that this exercise in introspection proved to be a revelation. They report finding a new kind of strength for themselves in the process of helping their daughters. One way to put that new strength into action is to share with your daughter two or three things you like about yourself. And at dinner after a day when you and your daughter did something together that you're proud of, be sure to mention that.

After some experience with validating yourself, try this activity with your daughter: Each of you will write a biography of yourself and a recommendation letter for yourself. That is, write about yourselves in the third person as though someone else were doing the composing. ("Jane Doe, a ten-year-old in Mr. Slate's fifth grade at Anytown Elementary, won the state spelling bee in 1997 after competing with hundreds of youngsters from all over Ohio. Jane is also a gymnast who . . ." etc.) For most of us, this is surprisingly difficult. It's not hard to praise the achievements and laudable qualities of other people, but saying wonderful things about ourselves can make us squirm. However, once you've done it and read the words out loud, you and your daughter will experience a rush of healthy pride in just exactly who you are.

However, each of you may also be taken aback by some of things you wish you could have put down. If so, resolve to do something about that situation. Look around for ways you may not even have thought of to utilize your gifts and gumption. Listen to the joyous words of Betsy Schoenfeld, a fourteen-year-old from Bountiful, Utah, who sees herself as capable of succeeding in just about any career she chooses:

Last year on Take Our Daughters to Work day at my mom's job, the theme was "The Sky's the Limit in Your Career Path." Little did I know the many places this path would lead me that day! We started with a tour of the Comprehensive Emergency Management Department. We got to see what would happen if there was a major disaster in Utah and how people would be helped because of this special technical computer room. I decided I wanted to be a specialist in emergency management! But before the day was over, I had also decided that I wanted to be a computer technician or pro-grammer . . . the governor of Utah . . . a horticulturist . . . a lawyer . . . a teacher . . . a veterinarian . . . the director of state finance . . . executive director of a not-for-profit organization . . . and a firefighter!

During the final session, I was invited to introduce the championship firefighter. It was the first time I ever got to speak in public. I went up to the stage and read the in-troduction into a microphone in front of a full auditorium and I didn't even make a mis-take! Everyone said I did a great job. Maybe I should be a public speaker. . . .

That's the kind of confidence every girl needs in order to step right up and be a "public speaker" for herself. Try this with your daughter. Go back to the biographies you wrote about yourselves and edit them so they become introductions, like the one Betsy read when she was asked to present the firefighter. Now improvise a microphone—a soup spoon will do for a prop here—and have your daughter read her words as though she were introducing herself. Get her an audience for this ex-ercise—her father, her brother, her grandmother, her best friend, any-body you can scare up. If you have a video camera, use it to capture this moment. Particularly if she is nine or ten now, she'll benefit later on from watching the girl she was. And whatever her age, she'll gain con-fidence as she lets people know what's good about her.

Activity: I Let People Know What's Good About Me

The biography, the letter of recommendation, and the introduction go in this chapter of her book.

Resource

Expect the Best from a Girl, That's What You'll Get, a public service campaign from the Women's College Coalition and the Ad Council, 125 Michigan Ave., NE, Washington, D.C. 20017
(800) WCC-4-GIRLS; (web site) http://www.academic.org.

36

Taking Charge Is Not the Same as Being Pushy

At about the age of three, the desire to be first in line comes over children of both genders with great force, as any nursery school teacher will tell you. Assigning a "line leader" each day, and keeping careful track of who has had a turn and who is still waiting for one, is common practice in early education, and all but the most agonizingly shy child is eager to take on the leadership role. Observe a group of preschoolers when the leader of the day is about to be chosen and you see little faces quivering with anticipation. Then when the leader is designated, you see a huge smile from him or her—and barely concealed envy from all the others. This same urge to be in front of the pack stays with children throughout grade school, although as we have discussed earlier, sometimes subtle gender inequity behavior from teachers and other adults begins to erode girls' confidence even during those tender years.

But as adolescence approaches, a dramatic shift occurs. Girls start to pick up on cultural cues that tell them that to be a leader is to be "unfeminine." The adjectives "bossy" and "pushy" are applied to girls who want to be in charge, whereas boys are praised for showing leadership qualities. And of course, the stereotype of the "lady boss" is still too often negative, portraying her as unattractive, domineering, whip-cracking, greedy, and generally not the sort of person you'd want to grow up to be.

Given all this, it's no wonder that girls are underrepresented in leadership positions such as student council president. And it's no surprise either that girls who have learned to take a back seat grow into women who stay there, and that boys who have learned to put women in their place grow up to be men who keep them there. According to a 1996 report from the U.S. Department of Labor Women's Bureau, in corporate America women hold just 2% of the power positions, no matter how you define them—by title, by paycheck, or by responsibility for the bottom line. This is even more disturbing in light of the fact that women make up a full 46% of the workplace today—and according to educated projections, by the year 2005, two out of three new workers will be women and women will comprise 48% of total paid workers. True, women did pass a milestone in the boardroom in 1996, holding for the first time more than 10% of the directors' seats at the nation's 500 largest companies. Yet of these same companies, only 61% can count even one woman among their top five earners or can say that 25% of their officers are women. And only 13% can do both.

> When our daughters ask why they may never see a woman president . . . we have no good answers for them. That's because there are none.
>
> Anna Quindlen

This means that while we've come a long way, we have a very, very long way to go. Women constitute a huge talent pool, a tremendous natural resource that is not being tapped with anything like the regularity that it should. The "glass ceiling" and "sticky floor" are still very much in evidence, and women are still not rising in any significant numbers to high-ranking positions. One good way to change this is to give today's girls what their mothers never had: An image of female leadership that is strong and positive and inspiring. We need to show girls that taking the helm is not a masculine trait and not a male birthright, and that being in charge is not at odds with being female in every good sense of that word. We also need to help boys grow into men who can work not only *with* but *for* women who deserve positions of power.

You can start the revolution at home. Read the book listed at the end of this chapter aloud with your daughter and with your son as well. After each chapter, discuss with the children how the girls and women behaved as leaders and what they accomplished.

Activity: I Am a Good Leader

Have your daughter record, in words and pictures, anytime that she is in a leadership position at school or in her extracurricular activities.

Resource

Girls and Young Women Leading the Way: 20 True Stories About Leadership, by Frances A. Karnes, Ph.D., and Suzanne M. Bean, Ph.D. (Minneapolis: Free Spirit Publishing, 1993).

37

Don't Stand for Sexual Harassment

Mindy, a blossoming thirteen-year-old, came into the kitchen where her father was putting out the fixings for a lasagna recipe the two of them liked to make together. "Hey there, how's my sunshine?" he said, but his daughter only managed a slight shrug in response. "Something wrong?" the father asked, and Mindy shrugged again. Wisely, the father didn't press her, but let her chop tomatoes in silence for a while. Finally Mindy said, "There is this totally gross guy who sits behind me in English class, and he thinks it's a riot to snap my bra. I've been trying to ignore him, but today, when I got up to walk out of the room after the bell rang, he patted me on the butt and said, 'Nice ass!' It was so disgusting!"

Mindy is not alone. According to a 1993 Harris Poll commissioned by the American Association of University Women (AAUW), 85% of girls say they have been sexually harassed during their school lives. The larger lesson here, however, is that harassment is often only the beginning in a chain that goes from butt patting to date rape to wife battering. In their 1993 book *Secrets in Public: Sexual Harassment in Our Schools,*

Nan Stein, Nancy Marshall, and Linda Tropp show that harassment brings with it what they call a "hidden curriculum." That is, girls internalize the idea that they are in danger and they begin to *expect* to be victimized. Consequently, they begin to function at less than optimum levels in all areas of their lives.

The AAUW report, entitled *Hostile Hallways: The AAUW Survey on Sexual Harassment in America's Schools,* confirms this. The study showed that sexual harassment disrupts girls' education. After being harassed, one in three girls doesn't want to go to school or speak up as much in class. More than one in five girls score lower on a test or paper or drop out of an activity. And two in ten girls doubt whether they have what it takes to graduate from high school. Even worse, a profile published by 9to5, The National Association of Working Women, showed that when sexual harassment goes unchecked in schools, girls may come to expect that it will also be tolerated in the workplace. The same survey documented that from 40% to 65% of working women have been sexually harassed at work.

Similarly, a 1997 study done by the Working Women's Department of the AFL-CIO reports that *respect* is a word working women use again and again to describe what they want. In response to an open-ended question asking what the biggest problem they face is, many cited lack of respect. Sexual harassment is also related to respect. 78% say 'punishment for sexual harassment' is very important. But 35% say this protection is not currently provided by their employers.

What, exactly, is sexual harassment in a school setting? The behavior Mindy told her father about certainly qualifies. While harassment has been "normalized" by a centuries-old nursery rhyme ("Georgie Porgy, pudding and pie / Kissed the girls and made them cry"), it remains degrading, and as Mindy put it, "disgusting." Other examples of harassment that girls encounter include sexual rumors ("She's a slut"), remarks about sexual orientation ("Hey, lesbo!"), peeping toms in the gym dressing room, flashing, and being cornered or backed up against a wall and forced to kiss. More recently, cities like New York have reported a rash of so-called "whirlpooling," in which boys surround a girl in a swimming pool, pull her suit down, and touch her.

If your daughter confides in you that she has been harassed, your first obligation is to take her seriously. Reassure her that she does not deserve to be treated with such disrespect and that she absolutely does not need to put up with this behavior. Guard against inadvertently blaming her in any way or implying that she "asked for it." Society is all too willing to do that by giving her the idea that there's something inherently wrong with being a girl, since being a girl is really all it takes to attract the attention of boys who are bent on harassment. Your daughter has usually not been singled out because she's especially pretty or voluptuous, nor because she has a come-hither smile or a flirty giggle. The normal and healthy behavior of a lively girl as she interacts with nice boys and learns the dance of male-female relationships doesn't deserve to be demonized.

Above all others, what has been forbidden to women is anger, together with the open admission of the desire for power and control over one's life.

Carolyn Heilbrun

If your daughter is the victim of taunts, her first course of action might be simply to turn and walk away, indicating that she is not even going to dignify the action or comment with a rejoinder of any kind. Typically, boys get bored with girls who don't give them any reaction. However, sexual harassment needs to be stopped so that your daughter is not revictimized.

Be sure you back your daughter up. In Mindy's case, her father recommended that she should speak with the English teacher about having her seat moved and that she should also request that she not be assigned any group work with the boy in question. Both Mindy's father and the English teacher, a man, were enlightened and helpful. However, not every case can be handled so easily. Many women and girls have needed to go further. For example, in Portland, Oregon, a group of girls supported by a Ms. Foundation for Women grant organized against sexual harassment. Their group is called Sisters in Portland Impacting Real Issues Together (SPIRIT). Newspaper articles and TV broadcasts have covered their speak-outs and other events.

Elsewhere, at a gathering of mothers and daughters held at a women's college, one mother told a story about a teacher who wasn't as sensitive as Mindy's. In fact, he was the perpetrator. This mother first made sure her daughter was willing to take the steps necessary in order to stand up for herself. After that, the two of them spoke with another girl who had been harassed by the same teacher, and then they called that girl's mother. The mother said she didn't want to get involved because she was afraid her daughter's grades would suffer. In spite of that setback, the original mother and daughter were eventually able to gather enough evidence to take on the teacher's behavior. Dealing with sexual harassment, as this story shows, can be difficult. The behavior is about power, not sex, and as the mother who declined to participate makes evident, that power can be silencing. If girls are to take action, parents need to stand with them—and girls need to know what the realities of taking action are. Parents can help girls assess the risk if the behavior is something they believe needs to be corrected, and then identify possible alternatives.

Activity: "It's No Joke"

Have your daughter collect examples of times when sexual harassment is couched as a joke. She can write down examples from TV shows and movies, and she can collect clippings from magazines and newspapers. If she gets really outraged by something she sees or reads, encourage her to write to the TV station or publication. The letter can be included in this chapter of her book.

Resources

Sisters in Portland Impacting Real Issues Together, 5806 North Albina, Portland, OR 97217; 503-283-5340; fax 503-283-1289; (e-mail) massaction@ igc.apc.org.

Tune in to Your Rights: A Guide for Teenagers About Turning off Sexual Harassment, from the University of Michigan, Programs for Educational Opportunity; 313-763-9910.

Powerplays: How Teens Can Pull the Plug on Sexual Harassment, by Harriet Hodgson (Minneapolis: Fairview Press, 1996).

Sexual Harassment: High School Girls Speak Out, by June Larkin (Toronto: Second Story Press, 1994).

Get Smart: What You Should Know (But Won't Learn in Class) About Sexual Harassment and Sex Discrimination, 2nd ed., by Montana Katy and Veronica Vieland (New York: The Feminist Press at CUNY, 1993).

38

Learn to Fight Back

Girls in today's world need a sense of power and personal control. Studies show that one way to give your daughter more security in her own body is to have her take a self-defense course. It is well-documented that girls and women who have taken courses walk differently, more commandingly, and are attacked less often. Also, girls who know how to protect themselves simply feel better about themselves in general and thus do better in school and in social settings as well. That is why a self-defense course is invaluable even if your daughter never finds herself in a perilous or compromising position.

And if she does ever face an attacker, she can assess the strength, the skills, and the knowledge she has to defend herself. Sadly, the chances that she might need to do that are pretty high. According to the most recent statistics available, females under the age of eighteen account for 51% of rape victims, although they make up only 25% of the nation's female population. As many as 19 million girls and women have been the victims of date rape in the United States. Add to that the increased incidence of muggings, domestic violence, stalking, and murder, and a very grim picture emerges. America is now the most violent country in the world, with twenty times the homicide rate of Western Europe and forty times the Japanese rate, as well as twenty times the number of rapes reported in Japan, England, and Spain. And a 1993 study by the American Psychological Association showed that teenagers are 250% more likely to be the victims of crimes than are adults.

Obviously, you want to protect your daughter. However, for a mother, this very urge can backfire. Authors DeBold, Wilson, and Malavé put it this way: "Teenage girls share their mothers' fears of physical and sexual violence, yet with a sense of invulnerability, they act as if they continually think, It couldn't happen to me. While men create the dangers, it is mothers who most often are 'forced to be their daughters' jailers.' Girls usually discount their mothers' warnings and respond with anger and contempt to unwanted—and in their minds, unnecessary—limits on their freedom and independence. Mothers' fearful, but justified, efforts to protect their daughters, their implied and explicit injunctions to do as they do, and their daughters' angry realization that their mothers' powerlessness mirrors their own future all join to place an unbearable strain on a relationship between mother and daughter."

One way to get out of this double bind is to *join* your daughter in mastering some form of the martial arts. This will help both of you feel safe—an outlook that is particularly important to your daughter's psychological well-being as she begins to attract a new kind of attention from boys and men, both those she knows and those she doesn't. However, let her know that even if she has taken a course, she is not to blame if she doesn't

> **W**omen's strength is their ability to adapt, but also to fight back.
>
> Yuri Kochiyama,
> human rights activist

manage to fend someone off. She is not a failure and it is never her fault. She does need to have the *permission* to try to defend herself when she can. You don't want her to feel helpless, as did one young woman, quoted in the 1992 best-seller *The Day America Told the Truth*, by James Patterson and Peter Kim. The woman talked about being date-raped as a college freshman: "I felt I had been an unwilling participant and that the woman was always guilty until it had been proved that she had been knocked unconscious, or doped and mutilated, before being raped. It didn't occur to me that it was okay to hurt him, to kick him in the balls, or punch him in the eye. Good girls didn't do that."

The good-girl mind-set, unfortunately, can be what keeps girls and women from protecting themselves. But a self-defense course can help you and your daughter get past that attitude. Mary Pipher, who attended a self-defense course at the Y with her teenage daughter, Sara, describes the process this way in *Reviving Ophelia*:

We pair off and practice. Under crystal chandeliers, we attack each other and struggle to break free. At first we are wimps. We giggle and punch the air with gentle, womanly moves; we apologize for our accidental aggression. We have to be reminded to scream, to go for the groin and the eyes. Gradually we improve. We stop being ladylike and learn some power moves—the Iron Cross and the Windmill. We marvel aloud that these moves might really work. As we practice, Kit walks among us, correcting, coaxing, giving us something we have never had before—instructions on fighting back.

Resolve to make a mother-daughter project out of learning how to fight back. You'll both be better off and you'll respect each other more as well.

Activity: I Know How to Fight Back

Have your daughter write about her feelings as she learns self-defense. She can put in a picture of the two of you in class.

Resource

Center for Anti-Violence Education, 421 Fifth Avenue, Brooklyn, NY 11215; 718-788-1775; fax 718-369-3192.

BAMM/Impact Self-Defense, 800-345-KICK; (web site) http://www.bamm.org; (e-mail) info@bamm.org.

American Women's Self-Defense Association. Phone: 800-43-AWSDA. Self-defense materials; listings of self-defense programs in your area.

39

Real Women Make the Best Role Models

Girls are fascinated by real adult women because they want cues about what they will be like when they grow up. However, in our media-saturated society, girls also get bombarded with *unreal* images—not only of how a woman looks but also of how she behaves and how she's treated and what she can expect to do in life. Consider the ubiquitous Barbie doll, she of the wasp waist and outrageously generous bosom, who has been collected and cherished by millions of girls (and grown women) since her debut in 1959. Barbie has evolved somewhat over the years, and a 1997 incarnation has slightly more realistic measurements. Yet while this new-age retooling and such versions as Dentist Barbie are meant to give little girls an ambition beyond that of wearing stiletto heels and ball gowns, the fact remains that the primary image Barbie projects is one of a blond, gussied-up femme fatale. In fact, Tina Rosenberg, in a 1997 editorial for *The New York Times*, wrote that most outfits make the doll look like Oldest Profession Barbie. Since that role is definitely not what parents want their daughters to aspire to, what are we to do?

And what about the way women are so often portrayed in other aspects of popular culture? Television, for example, has a very bad record when it comes to depicting adolescent girls, according to a 1991 Ms. Foundation for Women report by Debra L. Shulz. Shulz writes that researcher Sally Steenland conducted several media studies for the National Commission on Working Women of Wider Opportunities for Women, including *Growing Up in Prime Time: An Analysis of Adolescent Girls and Television* (August 1988) and *What's Wrong with This Picture: The Status of Women on Screen and Behind the Camera in Entertainment* (November 1990). Her 1990 report noted that the only age group on TV where females outnumber males is children under thirteen. Steenland also said that teenage girls on television are rarely the focus of a show's plot, unlike boys, whose "rites of passage" are seen as inherently more interesting and real than those of girls.

Similarly, a front-page article in the May 1, 1991, *New York Times* reported that the following season, there would be no children's shows on Saturday morning with female protagonists. The article emphasized—and seemed to accept uncritically—the views of many network executives who agreed that boys will not watch shows with female characters. Near the end of the article, the author did quote former AAUW president Anne Bryant's contention that the portrayal of girls on television contributes to girls' lower self-esteem but did not follow up by exploring solutions. And then there are all those advertisements in which women appear to be not much more than pretty props.

> **M**y funny, clever, bold, adventurous daughter is forming her gender ideas right now. I do what I can to counteract the messages she gets from her entertainment, and so does her father . . . It sure would help if the bunnies took off their hair ribbons and if half the monsters were fuzzy, blue—and female.
>
> **Katha Pollit, from The Nation**

Obviously, we can't get rid of Barbie (although your household can boycott her if you like). But you can write letters to the toy company, to TV producers, and to advertisers. This is a fine joint project for you and your daughter. Right now, companies want to reach girls, and you may be surprised by the extent of your influence. However, whether or not any changes are effected as a result of your efforts, you'll at least feel good about having had your say.

More important, though, is to talk with your daughter about not measuring herself by the unrealistic and often degrading standards of popular culture. Watch television with her, and then discuss the programs afterward. Also get her opinions about billboards along the highway and advertisements on TV and in print. Then have your daughter rewrite the scripts for the TV shows she finds offensive, or have her create a new one with a female character she could admire. In the same way, using colored markers or her computer, have her create advertisements that show girls and women in important roles saying smart things.

In addition, watch the reruns of *My So-Called Life*. This is a great antidote to unrealistic models of adolescent life. The show deals frankly with a diversity of race and class issues, sexual orientation, and the difficulties of facing conflicts. You can also rent videos of films with strong female characters and watch them together. Some good choices are *Fried Green Tomatoes, My Brilliant Career, Norma Rae, Steel Magnolias*, and *The Way We Were*. The editors of the *Daughters* newsletter suggest the following questions to help your daughter analyze the films with you, reprinted here with permission:

1) What choices did the female character make?

2) What was expected of her?

3) Did she break the rules or refuse to be "nice"?

4) If she got what she wanted, did she have to give up other things to get it? Was she wise?

5) If you were the writer or director, would you change the plot or ending?

Finally, get a copy of *Dreamworlds II*, a video available from the Media Education Foundation, 26 Center Street, Northampton, MA 01060; 413-586-4170. Prepared by Sut Jhally, professor of communications at the University of Massachusetts, the video examines the way women are portrayed in many rock-music videos. At the end, scenes of real sexual violence are interspersed with scenes from the music videos. You'll be hard pressed to tell the difference. MTV tried to stop distribution of this film. Thank goodness for the First Amendment. Be sure you and your daughter watch this video together and discuss its implications. Once again, remind her that she is a flesh-and-blood person with ideas and hopes and the potential to make a contribution to society.

She's a real girl with real brains and real ambitions. And *that's* why you love her so very much.

Activity: I Don't Buy That!

Girls are a huge consumer group and everyone—from toymakers to cosmetics companies to fashion designers—knows that. Why not teach your daughter to be an informed, choosy, and intelligent consumer? Have her collect advertisements from magazines and write down her reactions to ads she sees on TV. Have her question products she doesn't think do girls any good. Also, have her put peer pressure to work in a positive way by enlisting her friends in a campaign to change what they don't like. There's power in numbers, and it's also fun to work with others and get different opinions and ideas.

Resources

Girls Re-Cast TV^SM, a program of Girls Inc. 212-689-3700; http://www.girlsinc.org.

Where the Girls Are: Growing Up Female with the Mass Media, by Susan J. Douglas (New York: Random House, 1995).

Screen Smarts: A Family Guide to Media Literacy, by Gloria DeGaetano and Kathleen Bander (New York: Houghton Mifflin Company, 1996).

Children Now (Gender and Media Project), 1212 Broadway, Suite 530, Oakland, CA 94612; 510-763-2444; fax 510-763-1974; (web site) http://www.childrennow.org; (e-mail) children@dnai.com.

40

You Are Some Body!

Ours is a culture obsessed with "self-improvement." Cover lines from magazines and slogans in advertisements all scream at us to better ourselves, with the underlying implication that we're just not good enough the way we are. That message can erode the basic respect for her body that your daughter needs. Of course, it can erode your respect for your body, too. Do you find yourself making critical remarks about the way you look? Have you ever gone shopping with your daughter and blamed yourself instead of the clothes when something didn't look or fit just right? Most of us have. The trouble is that we're feeding right into that cultural obsession with self-improvement and giving our daughters the idea that a normal woman's body is not lovely and miraculous.

Our own messages about our bodies coupled with those from the media often lead our daughters to mistreat their bodies in a number of ways. A 1997 study by the Commonwealth Fund showed that girls as young as nine report dieting to lose weight. And up to 25% of adolescents—90% of them girls—say they binge and purge. The Commonwealth Fund survey found that nearly one in five girls in the ninth grade has symptoms of bulimia, and the figure doubles by the time girls are seniors in high school.

It is extremely important for your daughter's emotional and physical health that you talk with her about the unrealistic images she sees in the media. You don't want her to be seriously overweight, but she needs to understand that no amount of dieting or working out is going to change what her body basically looks like. If she's buxom, she's never going to rival Kate Moss in the stick figure department. And overzealous dieting can have dangerous consequences. The sud-

> **S**ometimes I think creativity is magic; it's not a matter of finding an idea, but allowing the idea to find you.
>
> **Maya Lin, artist**

den death in 1997 of twenty-two-year-old Boston Ballet dancer Heidi Guenther focused national attention on that tragic reality. Apparently, given the fact that Heidi was dangerously underweight and the discovery that she had been carrying a stash of over-the-counter laxatives in her bag, she had gone to perilous lengths to remain underweight, which she believed would get her the roles she wanted. Michele Vivas, a nutritionist who was on the staff of the School of American Ballet, says that seriously underweight people begin to use up the muscles of the heart. Heidi died of a heart attack. The autopsy was inconclusive, but anorexia was not ruled out as a possible cause.

Short of dying, however, young women who don't eat enough almost always suffer from a disorder called amenorrhea. In plain English, they stop getting their periods. Girls and women who do not have regular cycles can suffer stress fractures and a loss of bone mass.

Why would amenorrhea have anything to do with a stress fracture? If the condition goes untreated, a girl is likely to develop early-onset osteoporosis—a gradual reduction in the amount of bone-tissue mass. This debilitating condition usually doesn't afflict women until they go through menopause—the natural ending of menstruation that happens around the age of fifty. The reason for bone loss in girls with amenorrhea (just as in menopausal women) is a diminished supply of circulating estrogen—the hormone that, among other things, promotes bone density. Osteoporosis is progressive and, in later stages, may result in bones so fragile that the simple effort of standing erect can cause splintered hips or excruciatingly painful "crush fractures" of the vertebrae.

Osteoporosis is not the only problem associated with amenorrhea, however. A loss of fertility often results. When a girl starves herself, her system shuts down and she stops ovulating. Her reproductive system has gotten the message that she's too undernourished to support a pregnancy. Usually, if a girl gains weight, she will start ovulating again—but not always.

Three or more missed periods in a row should be taken seriously. In addition to gaining some weight, your daughter should be sure to get an adequate intake of calcium, the bone-building mineral. Skim milk and low-fat cheeses, as well as dark green vegetables such as broccoli and spinach, are rich sources. A supplement isn't a bad idea either. Regular weight-bearing exercise also promotes peak bone density, as long as your daughter doesn't overdo it. Disordered eating often goes hand in hand with extreme exercise regimens, so be on the alert for that behavior in your daughter.

Help your daughter do some research on good nutrition for growing girls and have her plan meals and snacks. She can create recipes, too, perhaps easy ones for the microwave so she doesn't skip an after-school snack. In addition, have her do some research about sleep needs. And since young girls are now the fastest-growing group of new smokers, have her educate herself about the dangers of smoking, as well as the dangers of alcohol and other drugs. She may also want to become a peer health educator in her school.

One way to help your daughter put her body image in perspective is to take her to an art museum. Show her how standards of female beauty vary from culture to culture and from era to era. Look at a Rubens painting together, and talk about how he appreciated the roundness and softness of the female form. She may say "Eee-www! That lady is gross!" but don't silence her. Ask her *why* she feels that way. Ask her if she thinks the woman Rubens painted felt gross or gorgeous. Also, rent some videos of films from times gone by. Talk about the fashions, the hairstyles, and the body types that were in vogue, and about how those trends have changed. Remind her that what's "in" today may well be "out" tomorrow and that trying to mold herself to society's dictates is to devalue herself as a person. Not that she can't fit in with her peer group, in the same way that you wear appropriate and up-to-date clothes to the office. But the point is that there is no one right way to look. Help her learn how to respect her body and to treat it right. Here, fathers can play an important role, since girls often equate being thin and beautiful with being attractive to boys. A father who counteracts that superficial attitude by talking about the real traits he values in women—talents, abilities, a strong character, compassion—can have a powerful effect on his daughter's self-image.

Which brings us to the subject of your daughter's sexuality. Girls who don't feel good about their bodies sometimes seek affirmation through early sexual activity. Remember the words of Marian Wright Edelman, president of the Children's Defense Fund: "The best contraceptive is a real future." The corollary is that girls without a sense of having a real future often get pregnant. A 1996 study by the Alan Guttmacher Institute showed that 13% of all births in this country are to teenagers. There are nearly one million adolescent pregnancies a year. Not only that, but the incidence of all sexually transmitted diseases is high for teenage girls, and AIDS is a genuine threat for our daughters today. Obviously, you simply cannot afford *not* to talk openly with your daughter about sexuality and reproductive health care. Dismissing the power of teenage passion is not realistic. Help her choose a gynecologist whom she likes and trusts. Planned Parenthood Federation of America can be of assistance. The contact information is 810 Seventh Avenue, New York, NY 10019; phone 212-541-7800; 800-829-7732 http://www.plannedparenthood.org.

The idea is not to have your daughter feel that sex is "bad." You want her to grow up to be a woman who will take full pleasure in her sexuality. But she needs to make wise choices and not be active before she's ready. A *Seventeen* magazine study done in conjunction with the Ms. Foundation for Women showed that both boys and girls say sex most often occurs because the boy wants it. Girls often agree to have sex because they want to please boys. Make sure your daughter understands that she should have sex when *she* wants to, with partners *she* chooses.

Take Our Daughters to Work day was not specifically designed to prevent teenage pregnancies, but building solid intergenerational relationships between girls and women and expanding girls' aspirations have turned out to play a big part in helping girls make healthy choices about their minds and bodies.

Activity: My Body Is Amazing

Share with your daughter the fact that women's bodies are inherently strong. Women get sick less often than men do, and women live longer than men. Women also excel at activities requiring endurance such as long-distance running and swimming the English Channel. Now ask her to think of her body as a superbly functioning machine and to list all the things her body does or could do, from clearing a hurdle to slam-dunking a basketball to having a baby to climbing a mountain. You want her to learn to appreciate her body for what it can accomplish, not just for what it looks like. Have her illustrate her ideas with sketches or photographs.

Resources

The Period Book: Everything You Don't Want to Ask (But Need to Know), by Karen Gravelle and Jennifer Gravelle (New York: Walker and Company, 1996).

The First Time, by Karen Bouris (Berkeley: Conari Press, 1994).

Teenage Health Care, by Gail Slap and Martha Jablow (New York: Pocket Books, 1994).

The Girl Within, by Emily Hancock, Ph.D. (New York: Ballantine Books, 1990).

The Body Project, by Joan Jacobs Brumberg, Ph.D. (New York: Random House, 1997).

It's a Girl Thing: How to Stay Healthy, Safe and in Charge, by Mavis Jukes (New York: Knopf, 1996).

41

Sports Are Not for Boys Only

Go to a Women's National Basketball Association (WNBA) or American Basketball League (ABL) game. Hear the cheers? They sound different from the cheers you're used to hearing at a basketball game. These are the voices of thousands of girls raised in an enthusiastic chorus to spur on their favorite professional female athletes. Sports have changed.

The debut issue of *Condé Nast Sports for Women* magazine hit the newsstands for the first time in October 1997, on the twenty-fifth anniversary of Title IX, the gender equity law that guaranteed a fair opportunity for girls to participate in physical education and sports programs. In that issue Gabrielle Reece, professional beach volleyball superstar, has this to say about being an athlete:

I started playing basketball in high school, then switched to volleyball. Both sports gave me a sense of discipline . . . and as my skills and physical conditioning improved, so did my attitude. . . . I became fluid and strong. . . . I felt great about my body because of what it could do. I stopped thinking about it as a purely aesthetic object and started thinking about it as a machine, something functional that could do things: lift, bend, hit balls.

More and more girls and women are feeling the same way. As Lucy S. Danziger, editor of *Condé Nast Sports for Women*, wrote: "At last count, the number of women and girls across the country who participate in sports had risen to more than 40 million. . . . These women are setting goals, and not just the tired one on the scale. They're concerned with being healthy and fit, but aren't obsessed with fitness. For them, being strong is the point."

Strong, we might add, not only in body but in spirit. Study after

I don't ride to beat the boys, just to win.

Denise Boudrot, jockey

study has shown that girls who participate in sports have higher self-esteem, lower rates of depression, and a more positive body image than girls on the sidelines. They are also more likely to earn higher grades, graduate from high school, stay off drugs, and avoid unwanted pregnancies. What's more, nearly 80% of women identified as key leaders in Fortune 500 companies participated in sports when they were girls. Female athletes are also physically healthier than are girls who sit it out. A mere four hours of exercise a week reduces the risk of breast cancer by 40 to 60%. On the flip side, a lack of exercise predisposes girls to heart disease, the leading cause of death in women, and increases the risk of osteoporosis.

Beyond the physical benefits, however, there are emotional ones. Donna Lopiano, executive director of the Women's Sports Foundation, maintains that sports help girls develop persistence. Being involved in athletic activities keeps girls from being quitters, and therefore helps them be effective in whatever they do. Lopiano also talks about how parents are much more likely to let mildly discouraged girls drop out of athletics than they are to let boys drop out. The message is clear: Your daughter needs all the support she can get from you and the rest of the family for staying in sports. Most girls are really interested in sports. We just need to encourage them to stay with it and to make sure they're enjoying what they're doing. Perhaps you could get involved at your daughter's school to make sure the tenets of Title IX are enforced. And on a more personal level, look at whether you are unwittingly keeping her from being a full participant in sports by giving her such responsibilities as baby-sitting for younger siblings after school. If so, look for another solution. She could share the responsibility with her brother, or the younger children could get involved in community or school programs in the afternoon.

Interestingly, the sooner a girl starts being involved in sports, the better. It is well documented that girls mature earlier than boys and need to be introduced to athletic activities earlier in order to maximize their development, particularly that of the central nervous system. According to a 1996 report from the Children's Television Workshop, the malleability of girls' nervous systems decreases markedly after the age of ten or eleven. In other words, early childhood for girls is the prime time for learning and internalizing motor skills. Little girls pick up movement skills more easily than older girls who have never been physically active do. Still, the old adage "better late than never" definitely applies here. The advantages of being involved in sports are too numerous to risk missing out on them, no matter what your daughter's age—or yours. In *Reviving Ophelia*, Mary Pipher notes, "Girls in sports are often emotionally healthy. They see their bodies as functional, not decorative. They have developed discipline in the pursuit of excellence. They have learned to win and lose, to cooperate, to handle stress and pressure. They are in a peer group that defines itself by athletic ability rather than popularity, drug or alcohol use, wealth or appearance."

> **I**f you can react the same way to winning and losing, that's a big accomplishment.
>
> **Chris Evert**

Even if your daughter isn't a born athlete, and even if she's a late bloomer, she needs to get out there and swim, climb, skate, row, pitch, catch, run, putt, stroke, spike, or bike her way to emotional and physical health. Team sports—soccer, rugby, softball—teach her not to be afraid to compete and they also teach her about group dynamics. Individual sports—track and field, horseback riding—help her strive for personal best. Involvement in sports is clearly a win/win proposition for your daughter as she grows up. Unfortunately, however, a quarter of a century after Title IX, high-school girls still drop out of sports at a rate six times higher than that of boys. A 1996 article in *The New York Times* cites as reasons for this trend such factors as unfair treatment by male teammates, the assumption by coaches and gym teachers that girls are not good players, inappropriate levels of challenge, lack of opportunities, and time conflicts with other activities.

Maybe so, but don't let your daughter become a statistic. Encourage her to find friends who share her interests and look for lots of different activities—kayaking, line and square dancing, racquetball, step aerobics, kickboxing, snowboarding. Also, let her know you care about her sporting activities. Show up for meets. Celebrate her successes. Support her in defeat. And for her good as well as yours, join her in being a sport. Take a rock-climbing class, run the rapids together, form a mother-daughter neighborhood softball league, learn inline skating. The possibilities are legion and you have everything to gain—a shared activity with your daughter, a heightening of mutual respect as you meet the challenges you'll face, a healthy body, and a healthy self-image.

One mother who backpacked with her teenage daughter deep into the temperate rain forest in Olympia, Washington, says the experience forged a bond that has never been severed. "We decided to do this on a whim when we were on vacation," the mother says. "There was a guide who took a group of us. I had no idea how hard it would be. I didn't realize how out of shape I was and I had to push myself to the limit. My daughter saw that, and she was so proud of me. We would come to a place where we had to ford a stream or climb a steep incline and she would be right behind me saying, 'You can do it, Mom, you can do it!' And I did do it, even though I was exhausted. But that night, in a tent by the River Hoh, I slept better than I ever had in my life. I woke up incredibly refreshed just as the dawn was breaking."

This mother says that back home, she and her daughter took up backpacking seriously, getting all the right equipment and joining a local group. "It changed our lives," she says. "I feel younger than I did five years ago and my daughter is growing into a confident and wonderful young woman. We talk easily with each other and we trust each other. The backpacking has absolutely had everything to do with all of that."

Activity: I'm a Good Sport

Have your daughter record in this chapter all of her sport-related activities, along with photos, awards, etc.

Resources

Jackie Joyner-Kersee: Champion Athlete, by Geri Harrington (New York: Chelsea House, 1995).

Going for the Gold: Shannon Miller, by Septima Green (New York: Avon, 1996).

Wilma Unlimited: How Wilma Rudolph Became the World's Fastest Woman, by Kathleen Krull (New York: Harcourt Brace, 1996).

The National Association for Girls and Women in Sport publishes resources; 800-321-0789.

Swoopes on Hoops, a basketball training video for girls by Sheryl Swoopes, a top female basketball player; 800-458-5887.

Women in Sports: The Complete Book on the World's Greatest Female Athletes, by Joe Layden (Los Angeles: General Publishing Group, 1997).

42

Don't Play Dumb

The first semester of seventh grade, Jane brought home a report card full of C's and D's, along with teacher comments such as "Doesn't work to her potential" and "Seldom completes lab assignments." Jane's parents were flabbergasted. She had been a straight-A student until then, an eager little scholar who devoured books far above her grade level and always had a million questions. What happened, they asked her? Is junior high really that much harder than elementary school? Is there something we can do to help? A tutor, perhaps? But all Jane would say is, "I don't know." And then she went up to her room.

A little later, hoping she could draw her daughter out, Jane's mother went up and knocked on the door. Jane called out, "Wait a minute!" and then her mother heard muffled giggles before the receiver clicked into the cradle of the phone. Jane walked over and opened the door, being careful not to smear her freshly manicured nails. "What?" Jane asked, a challenge in her voice. "What do you want, anyway?"

"Just to talk," her mother said.

"About my grades, right?" Jane said defiantly.

"Well, yes," her mother said helplessly. "You've always worked so hard in school."

Jane let out a little snort of a laugh. "Yeah," she said. "Jane the Brain." Then the phone rang and she lunged for it. "Hello?" she said, her voice sweet and lilting. "Yeah, um, look, um, hold on a sec, OK?" Jane covered the receiver and whispered to her mother in her best darling-daughter tone, "Mom, puuhh-leeeze can we talk later? This is a really important call."

Her mother went back down to the family room, where Jane's father was waiting. "I think she's got a crush on someone," the mother said. "Any ideas about how we can keep her focused on her schoolwork?"

That's not an easy question to answer. Jane's mother was right in her assessment of the situation, of course, as she would confirm a day or two later when Jane was feeling a little more chummy and communicative. In their school district, the seventh and eighth graders were in the same building as the high-school kids. A ninth grader named Tom had shown an interest in Jane from the first day he saw her on the school bus in September, and before long they were sitting together on the bus every day, and he was carrying her books while they talked about anything and nothing. Tom, as it turned out, was a track star but not much of a student. "I didn't want to come off like a nerd," Jane said. "The kids really did call me 'Jane the Brain' in grade school, and I didn't care then. I kind of liked it. But I didn't want Tom to get the wrong impression. I wanted him to think I was cool."

Unfortunately, Jane's story is neither unique nor new. It is, in fact, one of the oldest stories in the world. Girls have long suspected that besting a boy academically is not exactly an aphrodisiac, and they have also watched plenty of women be careful to downplay their intelligence in deference to their husbands. Mary Pipher, in *Reviving Ophelia*, admits that she herself fell prey to the female tendency to feign mediocrity in the presence of a male. "Denny and I went to the A&W Root Beer Drive-In on Highway 81," she writes. "Then he asked about my six-week grades. I had made A's, but I said I had two C's and was worried my parents would be mad. I can still remember his look of visible relief."

In fact, girls' instincts are pretty much on target. In 1996, *Mademoiselle* magazine did an informal survey on the Internet, posing the question "Are men threatened by high-powered women?" The first response, which appeared within a hour of the posting, was from an eighteen-year-old male college freshman who said that he believed the majority of men his age are indeed put off by intelligent and high-achieving women, "especially if they're smarter than we are." Scores of responses followed, and while some men said they were the exception to the rule, most were blunt about the fact that they would not be comfortable in relationships with women who were more prominent or financially successful than they were.

This is not particularly good news, but at least the faceless anonymity of the Internet provided a way to get some men to be honest about the subject. Is there a solution? Obviously, a girl like Jane risks her whole future if she lets her grades slip in an effort to be "cool." And as anyone with common sense knows, telling a teenager (or an adult) that she is not allowed to see someone she's in love with simply fans the flame.

If your daughter is neglecting her schoolwork or skipping soccer practice, you need to help her get back on track. Preaching probably won't help, but letting her know about high-achieving women who are partnered with men who are proud of them will send her the message that it's possible to be true to herself and still have boyfriends. Famous examples of co-star couples are President Clinton and Hillary Rodham Clinton, Bob and Elizabeth Dole, Margaret Thatcher and Dennis Thatcher, and Jackie Joyner-Kersee and Bob Kersee (who is also her coach). Also, look to your own community for women who are active and accomplished and who also have husbands and children.

> **T**hink wrongly if you please, but in all cases think for yourself.
>
> **Doris Lessing**

The truth is that while a lot of boys are very competitive and do want to hold the position of superior being in a relationship, plenty of boys—the best and the brightest—are interested in smart girls who can join them in academic pursuits and in other areas as well. Boys growing up today know girls are going to work, and girls know girls are going to work. Any boy worth your daughter's attention is aware that he'd be shortchanging himself as well as her if he expected her to play dumb and not reach her full potential.

One young man, a senior in high school, had this to say:

My mom is a stockbroker and she makes more money than my dad, who's a high-school teacher. This was never a sore point with either of them, and my sister and I grew up with that model—that it's natural for a woman to do the best she can. Also my mom is a runner and she enters the New York City marathon every year. So anyway, I have always dated girls who are interested in lots of things, too. Right now I'm dating the president of the student council. She is also very athletic. We are taking a rock-climbing course together. It's awesome!

Listen up, the Janes of this world. There are good guys out there who will love you for who you really are. Mom and Dad, find ways to let your daughter know that fact, so she won't risk doing herself in for the attention of boys who simply aren't worth her trouble.

Activity: I'm Smart and Proud of It

Have your daughter keep track of times when she had the urge to play dumb, and how she caught herself. If she has a boyfriend who appreciates her for her brains and not just for her looks, she gets to put his picture here and write about him.

Resource

The Shelter of Each Other, by Mary Pipher, Ph.D. (New York: G. P. Putnam's Sons, 1996).

43

Girls Have Special Gifts

In his best-selling book *Emotional Intelligence,* author Daniel Goleman says that because girls develop facility with language earlier than boys do, "this leads them to be more experienced at articulating their feelings and more skilled than boys at using words to explore and substitute for emotional responses such as physical fights." Goleman's work, hailed as "the groundbreaking book that redefines what it means to be smart," shows that girls and women "experience the entire range of emotions with greater intensity" than males do, and he maintains that this is a big plus for females throughout their lives, whether in the workplace or in the home.

Similarly, anthropologist Helen Fisher, in her book *Anatomy of Love,* wrote, "Women are, on the average, more verbal than men. They are also better at picking up all sorts of nonverbal cues. And they are outstanding at networking. Before the computer, before the knitting needle, even before the bow and arrow, women also developed another business tool—arbitration. . . . Negotiating is a female skill."

Arguments and research about the differences between the sexes have swung like a pendulum—from Darwin in 1871, contending that men are born smart while women are born selfless . . . to Margaret Mead in the 1930s, insisting that it's all in how people are brought up . . . and back again in recent decades to a kind of middle ground in the nature-vs.-nurture debate. We now have quantitative studies that show that little boys have more spatial ability and an aptitude for things mathematical. Other research shows that little girls have better language skills, longer concentration spans, and more relational skills. However, experience has shown that the environment in which boys and girls are raised can have a profound effect, enhancing innate qualities and improving on those that are not so natural. In other words, girls who apply themselves can excel in mathematics just as boys can do well in writing.

However, since girls truly *are* better at some things than boys are, it makes sense to validate those gifts in the interest of raising girls' self-esteem. One young woman, now in her early twenties, recalls growing up with a brother two years older than she:

Now that I look back on it, I realize he was always in the resource room because he was dyslexic, but at the time all I knew was that I would walk into math class at the beginning of every school year and the teacher would say, "Oh, you're David's sister," and my heart would sink. There was no way I could live up to that. In seventh grade, David scored in the top 3% in the nation on the Johns Hopkins talent search for math and science! He got to go into the city for special classes at the Museum of Natural History as a result. Me? I could pull Bs in math if I went for extra help.

There was a lot I was good at, though, like I won first place in the speech contest in ninth grade, and there was other stuff, like all my friends called me "the counselor." They used to come to me to vent about their parents or their boyfriends or girlfriends and ask my advice. I just had a knack for that somehow. So my parents started joking around, saying like, hey, she's going to grow up to be the next Ann Landers. Everybody would laugh, but inside I would think, what's so darn funny? OK, so I'm not a genius like my brother. Lay off already!

The truth was, of course, that this young woman *is* a genius, but in her own way. You can do your daughter a favor by catching yourself when you put more value on her brother's accomplishments than on hers. For the record, the young woman we just heard from is now a writer, having blended her superior verbal skills with her intuitive gift for giving advice. She is currently writing a book for children about multicultural understanding—an endeavor that is surely no less impor-

> **M**en are taught to apologize for their weaknesses, women for their strengths.
>
> Lois Wyse

tant than her brother's work as a physicist. In other words, while you want to encourage your daughter to explore nontraditional career opportunities, and you certainly want to have her stick to her math and science courses in school, she shouldn't get the idea that the nurturing and helping professions or the arts are in any way less impor-

tant than some others. Unfortunately, they usually pay less, but teaching, social work, counseling, and nursing have great rewards on another level. Remember, the whole point is for your daughter to find out who she is and to discover what life she would truly love to live. She doesn't have to accept the value other people place on any given profession. Also, in a fortunate twist of fate, the relational skills in which girls excel are becoming crucial to the most important work of today and tomorrow.

In addition, going back to Helen Fisher's quote at the beginning of this chapter, bear in mind that some of the higher-paying careers, such as business administration, call for skills that women have in abundance. Dealing with people is a skill that women have had to develop and it serves women well in jobs that require management, group decision-making, and the handling of employees' personalities day in and day out. Here again, as your daughter is growing up, take seriously the traits she exhibits. It makes sense to help your daughter feel appreciated for the things she's good at, even though they are less tangible than solving a math problem.

Activity: I'm Good at Getting Along with People

Here is where she learns to congratulate herself for working well in a group or on a team, talking things over without pushing her agenda, having sympathy for other people, being able to put herself in someone else's shoes, feeling good about helping someone out. She should make a mental note of the times she handled a situation well, went out of her way to comfort someone, stopped a potential argument, and kept things running smoothly. Then back home she can write about that.

Resource

Emotional Intelligence, by Daniel Goleman (New York: Bantam Books, 1995).

44

Girlfriends Are Good Friends

The work of Carol Gilligan and Nancy Chadrow showed that in infancy and early childhood, girls acquire gender identification in the context of sameness, connection, and relationship because in most cases they are cared for by females. Boys, on the other hand, define their identity through a separation from female caregivers. As a result, girls move into childhood with stronger relational skills than boys do, and a greater capacity for empathy. Little girls form intense bonds with other little girls and they talk about their feelings with one another. Little boys typically form "hail fellow, well met" relationships based on action. They climb trees and throw balls and play video games, but they don't say a great deal to one another about what's going on inside their heads.

However, when girls approach adolescence, something happens. According to research done in a 1993 report entitled "Gender and Emotions," by Leslie R. Brody and Judith A. Hall, at about the age of thirteen girls begin to use tactics such as ostracism, vicious gossip, and indirect vendettas. DeBold, Wilson, and Malavé put it this way: "As girls enter the competitive world of dating boys, a mother can . . . encourage her daughter not to abandon her friends as girls trash each other. By letting a daughter know that keeping her commitments to girlfriends is important, a mother gives a daughter another way of thinking and behaving amidst the world of men's desires, which typically leaves girls defenseless." Wise words, because as Gilligan's work showed, during adolescence and adulthood, girls and women can find tremendous strength in attachment and friendship, and they need to feel part of a "web of connectedness."

This fact is corroborated by the work of Stacey Oliker, Ph.D., an associate professor of sociology at the University of Wisconsin, Milwaukee, and the author of *Best Friends and Marriage.* Oliker reports that her research shows that friendships are very important to women in the long run. "Women shore each other up and help each other figure out how to make marriage work, how to bring up children, how to navigate in the work world," Oliker says. "Men tend to have buddies. They play golf or they have a drink after work, but they don't talk as much as women do about their private lives."

> **P**erhaps we should share stories in much the same spirit that explorers share maps, hoping to speed each other's journey, but knowing the journey we make will be our own.
>
> **Gloria Steinem**

For your daughter's well-being, then, you need to guide her through the teen years so that she doesn't feel she needs to abandon female relationships or turn against other girls to curry favor with boys. Encourage her to spend time with her friends, listen when she wants to talk about a friendship that seems to be going awry, and let her see you relating with your friends in a positive and supportive way. Show her that you respect women in all kinds of roles and lifestyles and that you are not competing with other women or threatened by their successes. You can reinforce what she sees by talking about your experiences. ("I don't know what I would have done without Ann all these years. She's always been there for me. And we have so much fun together! I always call her when I need a lift.") One mother told us that she intentionally brought a woman friend into her family's life after she had two daughters. "I didn't want my daughters to grow up thinking a man had to be the central part of our family's life, or my life," she says. "I wanted them to see the value of women. And the woman and my husband became great friends as a result."

Women have long been one another's support and solace through the vicissitudes of marriage, divorce, abortions, pregnancies, and child-rearing. They have been there for one another, making life bearable, better, offering hope, sharing the wisdom of experience, bringing food and comfort when someone is sick or dies or has a baby. One way to achieve the goal of having your daughter maintain healthy, trusting, noncompetitive relationships with girls and women throughout adolescence and into her adult life is to help her find one or more female mentors. We've explored the mentor concept elsewhere, but this aspect of the relationship—that of a girl bonding with a woman who feels secure in her own level of achievement—is one that is not so readily apparent but is very important nonetheless. A mentor can give your daughter career advice and inspiration, but she can also make your daughter feel connected in a very positive way to a female she admires and aspires to emulate.

Activity: I Have Great Girlfriends!

Have your daughter write "character sketches" of her closest five or six friends, the way a novelist would in preparation for writing a novel. She should include all the wonderful traits and abilities each girl has and include one or two examples of times when each girl was a true friend and ways she's been a good friend to each of them—helping out or listening or being a shoulder to cry on. This chapter of your daughter's book can also include snapshots of her with her friends doing things together or mugging for the camera during a sleepover. In addition, she can put in mementos from times she has shared with her friends.

Resources

Girlfriends: Invisible Bonds, Enduring Ties, by Carmen Renee Berry and Tamara Traeder (Berkley: Wildcat Canyon Press, 1995).

Mad at Miles: A Blackwoman's Guide to Truth, by Pearl Cleage (Southfield, MI: Cleage Group, 1990).

45

Helping Girls Isn't Hurting Boys

No sooner had the evening rush hour traffic begun to inch its way out of Manhattan after the first Take Our Daughters to Work day than a chorus of thoughtful (and not-so-thoughtful) voices could be heard saying, "What about the boys?" Of course, as women who feel that changing girls' lives for the better will also benefit boys, we had included lesson plans for boys in the materials we designed for the Day. But the world is anxious anytime attention is focused on girls and tends to lose sight of the fact that what is good for girls is ultimately good for boys as well. Gender equity is not about one gender. Boys pay a price for gender stereotypes just as girls do. If we change female stereotypes, we change male stereotypes, too, and eventually everyone is better off. We feel proud that our work has had the effect of raising questions about boys—questions that have never before been asked—thus initiating a new and important dialogue about how boys' lives need to change.

In a 1997 article for *The New York Times Magazine,* Carol Gilligan responded to a reporter's question about her "new work—your research on boys" in this way: "I don't see it as new work. It's really an extension of the work I have been doing with women and girls. I noticed that there was an asymmetry between boys and girls. Girls are more at risk psychologically in adolescence, whereas boys are more at risk—more stuttering, more bed-wetting, more learning problems—in early childhood, when cultural norms pressure them to separate from their mothers." Gilligan went on to report that her preliminary findings from work done with Barney Brawer for the Harvard Project "Women, Psychology, Boys' Development and the Culture of Manhood" show that boys are surprisingly vulnerable. "Under the surface, behind that psychological shield, is a tender creature who's hiding his humanity," she says. "I often say about my own three boys, who are now grown, that I feel that the world muffles the very best qualities in them, meaning their sensitivity. . . . We have to build a culture that doesn't reward that separation from the person who raised them. . . . To shift our understanding of what it means to be a man and to be a woman is to think about how we work and how we love. And what's more basic than that?"

> **F**eminism: It's the expectations that parents have for their daughters, and their sons, too. It's the way we talk about and treat one another. It's who makes the money and who makes the compromises and who makes the dinner. It's a state of mind. It's the way we live now.
>
> Anna Quindlen

Indeed. This is the fundamental lesson that was learned by Ellador, the heroine of Charlotte Perkins Gilman's feminist utopian novels, *Herland* and *With Her in Ourland*, written in the early years of the twentieth century. Ellador's dream for America's future rests with the "swift-growing" women's movement, but in the context of a change that would benefit all of humanity. At the end of *Ourland*, she says, "At first I thought of men as just males—a Herlander would, you know. Now I know that men are people, too, just as women are."

As parents, we can go a long way toward bringing up both our daughters and our sons to know that females and males are all people, and not adversaries but allies.

Activity: I Don't Put Boys in Their Place

Have your daughter imagine that she and her brother, if she has one, or a boy who's a friend but not a "boyfriend," have gone on an outdoor adventure—one that is planned to last at least three days—with a group of friends and an adult guide. Your daughter and the boy somehow get separated from the group. Depending on your daughter's experience or on shows she's watched on the Discovery Channel, she can make up as wild a setting as she likes—a forest, mountains, rivers, whatever. She should describe what supplies she and the boy have with them when they get lost and what the weather is like. Now that the setup for the story is created, a pivotal event takes place. The boy trips (or steps on a bear trap, or his rappel rope breaks, or the canoe tips over and he smacks into a rock). The result is a pretty serious injury—a broken foot, a badly sprained ankle, a wrenched knee. The boy is in agonizing pain, and he can't walk. Now, have your daughter describe how she would expect the boy to behave and how she would expect herself to behave. Would the boy cry or would he stifle his sobs and try to "act like a man"? Would he admit that he's scared? Would he say he wishes he weren't alone with "just a girl," or would he say he's glad he's with someone he knows and trusts, someone brave enough to help him? And how would your daughter react? Would she panic? Would she start to cry? Or would she stay calm? How would she comfort the boy? And how would she solve the problem?

Now have her write a second story. In this one, she and the boy have a beloved dog. If the boy is her brother, it's the family dog. If the boy is a friend, then the dog is either hers or his but they both play with it all the time and love it. In the story, your daughter and the boy are romping with the dog along a country road that is seldom traveled. Out of nowhere, two things happen simultaneously—a car comes around a bend at breakneck speed, and a rabbit hops out of the bushes and onto the pavement. The dog darts out after the rabbit, and in spite of the fact that your daughter and the boy scream for him to stop, it's too late. He gets run over by the car and is killed. The car speeds away, leaving your daughter and the boy alone. Now, as in the first story, have your daughter go on from here and describe her emotions and her display of emotions, the boy's emotions and his display of emotions, and how they deal as a team with the situation they're in.

When she has finished her stories, read them and talk about them with her. Also, ask her, "Where do we get our messages about men and women in the world?" Here is another opportunity to examine the TV shows and movies she sees and the magazines she reads. See if she can pinpoint certain shows, ads, or stories that reinforce gender stereotypes and that ignore the truth about how males and females can get along and help each other throughout life.

Resource

Boys Will Be Boys: Breaking the Link Between Masculinity and Violence, by Myriam Miedzian (New York: Doubleday, 1991).

46

Work for All You're Worth

In 1868, Susan B. Anthony said, "Join the union, girls, and together say 'Equal Pay for Equal Work.'" One hundred thirty years later, white women in this country still earn only 75 cents for every $1 white men make. Black women earn 63 cents and Latinas earn 56 cents. Even when women hold the same jobs as men, they don't earn the same pay. Whether a doctor or lawyer, an elementary school teacher or secretary, a truck driver or waiter, a man is likely to take home more money than a woman in an identical position, according to a 1996 U.S. Department of Labor report. Over a lifetime of earnings, women forfeit on average $420,000 in salary and pensions because of unequal pay.

But that's only part of the story. Women are also still concentrated in low-paying jobs. More than 60% of women working year-round and full-time get paid less than $25,000 annually. More than one in four working women have administrative support jobs or clerical jobs, with 1994 median weekly earnings of $374 per week—20% to 30% less than women in nontraditional fields.

Not surprisingly, the survey entitled "Ask a Working Woman," conducted in 1997 by the Working Women's Department of the AFL-CIO, revealed that the top concern of women who responded is equal pay. Almost unanimously (99%), working women describe equal pay as important—and 94% say it's very important. Not only that, but vast numbers of the women who work outside the home, particularly part-timers, report going without basic benefits such as paid sick leave, health coverage, and pension plans. In response to an open-ended question that asked them to describe the biggest problems facing women at work, the survey participants cited lack of equal pay, low pay generally, gender discrimination, and the "glass ceiling."

Women, clearly, are still not working for all they're worth. This deplorable situation is not a female problem. It is a problem for everyone of all ages. The AFL-CIO report and a report from the Families and Work Institute both show that families depend on working women. Nearly two-thirds (64%) of working women report that they provide half or more of their household income. In addition, 41% of working women head their own households—they are single, divorced, separated, or widowed—and 28% of them have dependent children. In other words, there is simply no one of any gender who has a reason to be *against* paying women what they deserve to be paid. Yet ironically, the rallying cry of Susan B. Anthony is still as necessary today as it was well over a century ago.

What, then, is the solution? The women who responded to the AFL-CIO survey overwhelmingly agree in principle with Anthony's exhortation to "join the union." A full 79% say the best way to solve problems in the workplace is for women to "join together and work as a group," and 75% endorse labor unions. These are issues that you and your daughter—as well as other family members, given the universality of the concerns—need to discuss together. In the 1960s and 1970s, the phrase "consciousness raising" came into common parlance, and it needs to be resurrected as a concept whose time has come again. Your daughter is part of a brave new generation of girls entering womanhood. The 1970s are ancient history to her, and yet many of the most basic problems for women, those having to do with our very livelihood, remain unresolved.

To be blunt, money may not buy happiness, but it is essential not only to a girl's self-worth but also to her ability to get the most out of life. And it's not just the matter of equal pay that you need to discuss with your daughter. It's the romantic fallacy that she could collapse into the arms of a strong man and never have to (or want to) take care of herself again. In fairy tales, characters such as Snow White and Sleeping Beauty go into a dormant state (not unlike real girls at adolescence), and they wake up when it's time to marry the prince. In life, that is seldom the scenario, at least not as we approach the turn of a new century. However, the great female thinkers of a century or more ago already knew the truth in their bones. Mary Wollstonecraft wrote in 1792: "If women be educated for dependence; that is, to act according to the will of another fallible being, and submit, right or wrong, to power, where are we to stop?" And George Sand (the pseudonym of Amandine-Aurore-Lucile Dupin, Baronne Dudevant) had this to say in 1856: "In our wholly fractious society, to have no cash at all means frightful want or absolute powerlessness." Similarly, in 1912, the novelist Willa Cather penned these words: "No one can build his security upon the nobleness of another person."

With that in mind, give your daughter the incentive to look toward making a living for herself by starting her right now with some hands-on money management activities. In Chapter 25, we discussed the benefits of having your daughter get involved in an entrepreneurial pursuit. Now help her with the nuts and bolts of handling her finances. Actually, dealing with money is a lot of fun. Paying bills is only a drudgery when you always have too much month at the end of your money. But if you're reasonably solvent and you learn the ins and outs of budgeting, then making and managing money becomes a heady experience. Let your daughter have a taste of it now, and she'll never want to be without it.

In sum, when it comes to the larger arena of the inequities women still face regarding pay in the workplace, get your daughter involved and active: Share with her the bald facts at the beginning of this chapter and encourage her to ask mentors questions about pay and unions, as well as to try her hand at writing on the topic for the teen magazines mentioned back in Chapter 33. But on a more personal level, teach her to handle money. Get her a bank account in her own name, explain how to write and endorse checks, how to read a bank statement, and how to reconcile a check ledger. Also, teach her the joy of compound interest and explain how mutual funds and stocks and bonds work. If you need to bone up, check out the resource list at the end of this chapter. Remember that high finance is not just for the big boys on Wall Street. Did you know that if your daughter were able to put away $5 a day from the age of twenty-five on, she'd be a millionaire by the age of sixty-five? Of course, inflation would make that cool million a little less cool, but hey!

One thing you'll be accomplishing by having your daughter get really involved in her financial life is that you'll be showing her that math—well, all right, arithmetic—is relevant in her life right this minute. And another is that you'll be letting her know how thrilling it is to have the power of the purse strings. Once she knows that, she'll never want to let go.

Activity: I'm Going to Work for All I'm Worth

Have your daughter do some thinking about ways of making "equal pay for equal work" a reality. This is a good place for her to brainstorm with her friends. She can write down her ideas. Also, she can join a Junior Achievement club and write about her experiences for this chapter of her book. JA educates young people about business, economics, and what it takes to be successful; (web site) http://www.ja.org.

Resource

Get a Financial Life: Personal Finance in Your Twenties and Thirties, by Beth Kobliner (New York: Fireside, 1996).

47

Women Are Good Providers

As we have seen, research has shown that both boys and girls growing up today know that girls are going to work outside the home. After all, the majority of children today have mothers who do. Fewer than 18% of today's families have a single breadwinner and a person who stays in the home. The majority of families are dual-worker ones. Even so, girls want to know the answer to the question "How do you combine a family and a career?" There is, of course, no one answer. There are many ways to restructure paid work and reward work in the home and community that is unpaid. But ideal solutions are not yet in place, and many families are still limited to choices that are not perfect. Those who can afford to do so hire help or send children to day-care centers. Some parents rely on extended family members. Some couples share a job so that they can each be home with the children at some point during the day. Many parents also take advantage of flextime, which a lot of companies now offer so that people can be available to care for children before and after school. Other companies offer compressed workweeks, telecommuting (as long as the employee has child-care arrangements), and various forms of parental leave. Even so, the

United States lags behind other industrialized nations in offering ways to support working parents.

Your daughter needs to look at a lot of models, ask a lot of questions of different people who have made different choices, and make some choices of her own.

Share with her the following eye-opening statistics from the 1997 survey by the Working Women's Department of the AFL-CIO:

- 62% of working mothers with children younger than six say that child care is very important to them. But only 13% of these mothers have jobs that provide child care.
- Of working women with children younger than twelve, 56% say child care is very important. But only 11% have jobs that provide child care.
- African-American (47%) and Hispanic (50%) women are the most likely to want child care but not have it.
- 47% of working women call elder care very or somewhat important, but only 8% have it provided through their jobs.
- Women look to many institutions for more help in solving problems at work, including employers and businesses (96%), working women's organizations (92%), government (79%), community and civic groups (76%), and labor unions (75%).

However, while women who work outside the home today have problems they would like to have addressed, they see their paid work as helping their family. Women are good providers today in every sense—they provide nurturing and they provide economic support. The 1995 report by the Families and Work Institute showed that even though they're concerned with pervasive time pressures, a majority of women would not give up their jobs. What's more, women are optimistic about the opportunities for the younger generation of women. By a margin of six to one, they expect the younger women to have more rather than fewer opportunities than they have had. Be sure your daughter gets that potent message and does everything she possibly can to make the promise a reality for herself—and for her peers.

Activity: I Could Take Care of My Family

Have your daughter list the ways she would take care of her family in the future. Her list might include earning money. Then have her write about her childhood experiences vis-à-vis having a mother who did or did not work outside the home, full-time or part-time. If she went to day care, did she enjoy it? Was she cared for by a grandmother? Was that fun? Did her mother not work outside the home? Was she happy about that? She can also interview her friends, both boys and girls, and get their take on the ways in which they were brought up, and do the same with her siblings and step-siblings of both genders. Now have her interview adults—friends, grandparents, teachers, mentors—about how their workplaces allow women and men to be parents. Maybe she and her friends would like to do a research project on companies' policies regarding such issues as family leave after the birth of a child, flexible scheduling, on-site day care, paid leave for family emergencies, and benefits packages, including health, disability and life insurance, and retirement plans. A good source is the annual report by *Working Mother* magazine on the one hundred best companies. Then have her put forth some ideas about how she thinks she would like to plan her life, including a time sequence, so that she can do all the things that matter to her.

Resource

Distinguished Women of Past and Present web site

This site showcases women who have contributed to our culture in many different ways and allows you to search for individual biographies either by name or by field of activity. A majority of these role models have had both careers and families.

http://www.netsrq.com/~dbois/index/html

48

Share and Share Alike

In 1972, the late Jessie Bernard, the grande dame of American sociology, wrote in her now classic book *The Future of Marriage* that women tend to enter matrimony with a sense of responsibility, while men go into the commitment with a sense of entitlement. A lot has changed in the twenty-five years since then, but every woman who has ever picked up her partner's dirty socks off the floor knows what Bernard meant. And no, this is not a trifling issue, but an extremely significant one that your daughter should be aware of.

Author and activist Letty Cottin Pogrebin, in her book *Growing Up Free*, cites one study that found women to be doing 80 to 95% of all household tasks. She also referred to another sample that revealed that the task assignments for boys and girls in the vast majority of families are sex-differentiated: girls set the table, do the dishes, dust, and make beds, while boys are asked to empty wastebaskets, take out the garbage, shovel walks, and wash the car.

Regarding these findings, Pogrebin states, "How the labor of the family enterprise is split has been shown to have long-term effects on children's competence formation, their ability to surmount stereotypes, and their lifelong interests and occupational choices. If parents' home chores are sex-typed and if they assign their children to comparable tasks, they are in effect apprenticed to sex roles. Thus housework is *not* trivial. It tells children how valuable males and females are, what their time is worth, and what they can expect to be and do in this world."

Close to two decades after Pogrebin wrote those words, research shows that, on average, employed women *still* work two more hours per day in the home than employed men do. That, as any teenage girl would be quick to point out, is not fair. In the same vein, the 1995 report from the Families and Work Institute presented as a key finding the fact that regardless of their employment status, almost nine in ten women agree that they are responsible for taking care of the people in their families. Another finding was that nine out of ten women report experiencing a "time famine."

> **S**port strips away personality, letting the white bone of character shine through. Sport gives players an opportunity to know and test themselves.
>
> **Rita Mae Brown**

None of us wants to send our daughter the message that what she has to look forward to as an adult is a life fraught with overattention to the needs of everyone but herself, and a daily schedule that guarantees being overtaxed, exhausted, and deprived of leisure and personal pleasure. Pulitzer Prize–winning author Nancy Rubin posits that in the millennium to come, changes in our current gender construct may well come to pass. But, she argues, "as women, as individuals, as rational human beings, can't we begin to make these changes happen today—not by blaming ourselves for our 'inadequacies' as imperfect mothers . . . not by becoming man-hating radicals, but by working with men as well as women, by asserting our rights to be fully human, as well as to be mothers?"

And yet as recently as 1997, in the wake of the so-called "nanny trial" involving a British teenager accused of killing an eight-month-old baby who was in her charge, a flurry of articles and television shows pointed the finger of blame at the baby's working mother. The mother, an ophthalmologist, works only part-time and often comes home for lunch, but she was seen by many as being at fault for having a live-in au pair assume some of the care of her young children. The father in the case came under no such fire. And even the august *New York Times*, in response to all the fuss, saw fit to run an article on the front page of the business section probing the question of working-mother guilt, with quotes from women saying they tell their children they work for the money, since mentioning personal gratification or esteem seems like a "selfish" reason to be employed outside the home.

Our culture is hard on women. In the wake of the legislation regarding "workfare," op-ed pages were filled with essays insisting that welfare mothers should indeed be required to work. Yet when women who can afford to stay home choose to work outside the home, they are attacked as well. How much better it would be if our daughters could envision a future that would include a healthy and happy balance between self-fulfillment and caring for those they love, without criticism for the choices they make. And beyond that, our daughters should be able to look forward to lives in which they share and share alike on the homefront with their partners.

Activity: I Do My Share

Have your daughter list her responsibilities within the family, and those of other siblings as well. She may want to make suggestions for some changes, or think up ways the responsibilities could be divided more fairly, possibly with a rotation schedule so that one child is not always responsible for a certain task and so that jobs are not always assigned along gender lines. Particularly if she needs time for sports and other extracurricular activities, let her voice an opinion about whether she has been given more than her share of responsibilities.

Resource

The Second Shift: Working Parents and the Revolution at Home, by Arlie Hochschild (New York: Viking, 1989).

49

Do Good While You're Doing Well

When Cecil Rhodes established the annual scholarship program that each year provides thirty-two Americans with the opportunity to study at Oxford University, in England, he listed among the criteria for selection a "devotion to duty, sympathy for and protection of the weak, kindliness, unselfishness and fellowship." The current manual for would-be Rhodes Scholars puts it this way: "Rhodes clearly intended 'public duty' to be understood in the broadest sense: i.e., as referring to activities directed toward the welfare of others, and not solely to the holding of public office. . . . Rhodes sought Scholars who were more than 'mere bookworms'; he wanted their intellectual talents to be combined with concern for others. It is that blend of character with intellect to which the Selection Committee assign the highest importance."

Your daughter may or may not be a future candidate for a Rhodes Scholarship, but whatever she does, you want her to have that "blend of character with intellect." Compassion is a great energizer, and doing something that helps someone out always carries with it a fundamental feeling of worthiness and well-being. Be sure your daughter doesn't downplay the importance of the things she does for others, such as of-fering a kind word, sending a card or some flowers when someone is ill, or running a little errand or doing a chore for a person in need. All of these compassionate gestures combine to give a girl the sense that her life has meaning and that she is not just a kid cramming for an exam that everybody keeps telling her is so important. Acts of altruism ground your daughter and keep her from getting the idea that her life is noth-ing more than a frantic hustle and bustle, devoid of content.

Beyond that, being active in her school and community will also nudge your daughter out of the normal self-absorption of the adolescent years. Taking action for a worthy cause not only helps a girl to stop obsessing about whether every-body in the line for movie tickets is looking at her zits, but it also gives her a sense of her power to contribute to society and to change it as well. And as we have seen ear-lier, acting to effect change is a key component of resilience.

Service is the rent you pay for being.

Marian Wright Edelman

Another benefit of community service and volunteerism is that your daughter will get out of the junior-high and high-school setting for pe-riods of time and will mingle with people of different ages and differ-ent circumstances. This will go a long way toward doing some damage control for the effects of our age-segregated and class-segregated soci-ety.

As one privileged young woman who works once a week in the soup kitchen at her church said:

Before I started doing this, the only people I was in regular contact with besides my mom were all kids my own age. So I was just pretty much living in this fake world. We would see homeless people on the street, but they weren't real to us.

Then my mom suggested I should do some volunteer work. She had been working on an AIDS hotline, and she said she found it really rewarding, so she wanted me to get involved in something, too. She thought the soup kitchen would be a good place for me to start. I'll be honest with you. The idea of being there gave me the creeps. I was a total snob. But then when I started doing the work, I changed. There are single moth-ers with children. And there are old people who come and have stories to tell. They taught me fascinating stuff about other countries where they grew up. So what I'm say-ing is that this has opened me up and made me think about something besides my out-

fit for the homecoming dance. I do work hard in school, and I have goals, but work-
ing in the soup kitchen gave me a new perspective. I was so prejudiced before. I thought
I would just go through the motions with the people at the soup kitchen, but I ended up
loving the people there and learning from them. I'm a different person now.

In fact, this girl got so interested in her work at the soup kitchen that she eventually went a step further. She organized a speak-out at her school about the issues affecting people below the poverty line, and she got a canned goods drive going. Share this girl's story with your daughter and then look around for opportunities in your community for her to volunteer for. Also, see if she, too, might not go that extra mile and find an issue or a situation she could address with action—a campaign, a petition, a group of her peers dedicated to a cause. Some possibilities to get her started include helping out at the local hospital; volunteering as an aide in a child-care center or after-school center; working for the Red Cross; joining a youth group that is geared to community service; working in a battered women's shelter, a homeless women's shelter, or a shelter for runaway teens; and building a house with Habitat Humanity.

Activity: I Reach Out to Others

Have your daughter list her volunteer activities and write about her experiences. She can include illustrations and photographs of herself with the people she's helping.

Resources

Youth Service American (YSA) has launched a Fund for Social Entrepreneurs to invest in visionary young leaders who have bold, effective, and innovative ideas for national community service ventures. http://www.servenet.org

The Girls' Guide to Life: How to Take Charge of the Issues That Affect You, by Catherine Dee (Boston: Little, Brown and Company, 1997).

50

Parents Are People, Too

When a girl goes to work with her mother or father, she learns a great deal more than how to sell a product, track a meteorite, legislate law, conduct an orchestra, negotiate a raise, brainstorm, bandage, navigate, weld, compute, collaborate, sauté, or sew a seam. As we have already seen in conjunction with girls and mentors, a girl who is invited into a workplace gains an admiration for what adults do as well as a sense of being valued by someone who has taken the time to relate to her one on one. The same holds true of a girl-parent scenario, but there is another dimension involved—and once again it is a two-way interaction that benefits everyone concerned.

First of all, the girl's eyes are opened to the fact that her parents have responsibilities in a sphere beyond the home. She has always known that fact in the abstract, but witnessing the transformation of Mom or Dad into doctor, lawyer, or corporate chief—or butcher, baker, or candlestick maker—makes an indelible and very positive mark on her developing psyche. Like girls in an earlier, less age-segregated era, she sees her parents as part of the world at large. She incorporates into her image of them the roles they play as skilled, valued, and hardworking members of society, and she brings that image home with her. Until then, she has most often seen herself and her siblings as the center of a universe in which Mom and Dad exist to cuddle and coddle and fix meals and read stories and roughhouse—and later, to enforce curfews and keep tabs on the dating scene and limit telephone time and insist on homework being done. Now she has a broader view. Here's the way some girls express this:

"Some things that my mom did [as a nurse] looked pretty complicated—for example, administering intravenous medications. I was, however, able to check a patient's extra-ocular movements, with my mom's guidance, of course. These experiences taught me that being a nurse isn't just taking orders from doctors. Becoming a nurse requires intelligence and a good education. I was at work with my mom for four out of the eight hours that she worked that day. When it was time to leave, I was exhausted. I looked over at my mom and she was still going strong! This made me realize that being a nurse is very hard work."

Gina Cohen, Bronson, Florida, age fourteen

"My mother is a Commercial Vehicle Officer 2 for the Washington State Patrol. . . . By watching my mom, I learned that no matter what sex you are, it shouldn't play a part in determining a job. If you really want a job, you can get it. My mom showed me this because she works in a male-dominated work environment. Not only did she pass the academy and become a WSO Officer, but she was just nominated Officer of the Year for her district, which is a great accomplishment."

Melissa Kirkeby, Olympia, Washington, age fifteen

"Before my mother's work started having Take Our Daughters to Work day, I used to feel a little jealous of all the time she spends there, but now I see all the good things she does for people there and how hard she works. I look forward to my special day with my mom because I leave her job feeling proud of her and myself. She started out as a nurse's aide and worked her way up to RN supervisor."

Stacey Pouncy, New York, age thirteen

"My father puts our family's needs ahead of his own by waking up at 3:00 A.M., dri-
ving three hours, working the whole day, and driving three more hours home. Unfor-
tunately, it wasn't until I went with him that I realized how much he did for us."

Luxme Hariharan, Madison, Wisconsin, age fifteen

Beyond this acquisition of greater respect for their parents on the part of the girls, the second benefit of a parent-daughter day on the job is that the business world is forced to look at employees as family people in a real context. Policies like parental leave suddenly become real policies affecting real children. In this culture, that development is nothing short of revolutionary. Back in 1982, Dr. Donna Shalala, then president of Hunter College and now Secretary of Health and Human Services, gave a keynote address during which she said: "Employers not only don't wish to hear about it or know about it, they actively wish the worker's family didn't exist. . . . The family ties compete with loyalty to the company. If you must have a family, the prevailing attitude says, you must be a good enough manager so it presents absolutely no problem."

The occasion of Dr. Shalala's speech was the sixtieth anniversary of the Association of Junior Leagues at a symposium called "Women, Work, and the Family" at the Hunter College School of Social Work. That was a time when women were gaining a foothold in the mostly male workforce. In order to compete within the existing structure, they used such ploys as calling in sick rather than say they were going to a parent-teacher conference, or instructing the children never to call the office except in a dire emergency. What the women didn't realize was that the men they were emulating by putting job before family were aching to reverse the order of priorities themselves. It is well documented that fathers often feel more bereft when children leave the nest than women do, because they realize too late how much they missed. As one newly retired man told a reporter for the *Ladies' Home Journal* in 1993, "One day it hit me how sad it is that I suddenly have all this time on my hands and the [children] are gone. . . . When they were little, I tried to be a good dad. . . . But I didn't get to pal around with them much on a regular basis. . . . I missed a lot of their growing up." Here is a man who spent a lifetime providing for

You must know the story of your culture and be proud of your ancestors.

Romana Banuelos

children with whom he barely got to interact, in large part because he was not allowed to be what Marie Wilson calls a "public father." "When we started Take Our Daughters to Work day, fathers gave us feedback about how wonderful it was to be seen by their colleagues as fathers," she says. "Hard as it is to believe, men are often more punished for being public about their family responsibilities than women are. Men tell us they feel they have to hide their fatherhood. Some men said that their employers hadn't even realized they had children. But with the establishment of the Day, they finally had not just permission but a *mandate* to proclaim fathering as a part of who they are."

> **N**obody, but nobody/Can make it out here alone.
>
> **Maya Angelou**

And so girls stand to gain greater insight into their parents as people, and parents get a chance to go public about their roles as mothers and fathers, but there is yet another benefit that can be reaped when parents bring daughters into the workplace—and it may be the most important of all. Parents inevitably discover, when they assume the role of teacher-for-a-day by taking their daughters to work, that they learn something from their daughters. For example, girls who have been asked to review ads have changed whole advertising campaigns. Other girls have raised issues about race and gender and were heard in a way that adults had not. Also, at the MacArthur Foundation, girls have made recommendations for the so-called "genius awards" with refreshing points of view. And at the Ford Foundation, president Susan Beresford fielded questions from girls that were so perceptive that the parents in attendance looked at their daughters with new admiration. Many mothers and fathers have been emboldened themselves after hearing their daughters' courageous examples of speaking out. The girls give their parents an infusion of the clear-eyed, unspoiled spirit of youth. Without a doubt, everybody's a winner.

Activity: I'm Proud of My Parents

Each girl can change the title of this chapter to reflect the family she is growing up in. She might be in a two-parent family or a single-parent family. Maybe she's being reared by her grandparents or other extended family members. Maybe she's the daughter of a gay or lesbian couple.

Maybe she's adopted and would like to write thoughts about her birth parents as well as her adoptive parents. Maybe she is in a blended family. Whatever her situation, she can write about the adults in her life and about all the ways they care for her. Snapshots, of course, can be included.

Resources

Family Politics: Love and Power on an Intimate Frontier, by Letty Cottin Pogrebin (New York: McGraw-Hill, 1984).

51

Nobody's Perfect

Take Our Daughters to Work day, even though it has to do with going to places of business, has come to have almost a holiday feel about it. Girls and adults alike look forward to the occasion, now a permanent red-letter day on the country's calendar. And when that April morning finally dawns each year, everybody dresses up, and corporations large and small make sure everything is in order and that special breakfast and lunch menus are on hand. As the day goes on, people are excited and happy and on best behavior. Handshakes and smiles abound, flashbulbs pop, video cameras catch the action, and the media celebrates with articles and photographs and broadcasts about this astonishing nationwide event.

That's wonderful. Girls deserve the attention and thrive on it. They put pictures and mementos of the day in scrapbooks and they write in their diaries about meeting prominent people and having time with their parents and learning about opportunities they never knew existed. But let's be honest. Like any holiday, this one has an air of unreality about it. Precisely because it is designated as an extraordinary day, people and places seem larger than life, and indeed, everyone makes a superhuman effort to be as perfect as possible. That is one part of what is otherwise an inspiring message which you, as parents, need to temper. The image of the perfect still has a tenacious hold on most girls, and the closer a girl is to achieving this unhealthy goal, the more she must be encouraged to rail against it.

Nobody's perfect—not you, not your daughter's mentor, and not your daughter. Even the most accomplished of mentors has made mistakes, missed the mark, been rejected, suffered disappointments, locked the keys in the car, knocked over a glass at the dinner table, and forgotten how to pronounce a key person's name right before stepping up to the podium to make an important speech. Your daughter needs to know that. It will be a tremendous relief to her, not a disillusionment. She must not see the lives of those she aspires to emulate as a series of snapshots of perfection, like the photographs in an album. Who, after all, ever says, "Oh, honey, run and get the camera! The children are arguing again!" We take pictures of birthday parties and Christmas morning, not of tears and unmade beds and people with head colds blowing their noses.

And the media, of course, are just a commercial extension of that phenomenon. Does your daughter know that the food pages of glossy magazines are actually faked, with shaving cream substituting for meringue and water droplets sprayed on specially grown oversized fruits and vegetables that are in fact inedible? Does she know that models sit for hours while experts coax their hair into just the right styles and use professional makeup tricks to fool the camera? Does she know that when models wake up in the morning, they are just as puffy-eyed and pimply as the next girl? Talk about all of that with her and free her from the need to strive for perfection, which is an age-old form of tyranny over females.

> **B**e bold. If you're going to make an error, make a doozy, and don't be afraid to hit the ball.
>
> Billie Jean King

Reaching for an unattainable ideal dooms girls to feeling bad about themselves simply because they can never reach the standards they believe they must in order to be good enough. Think of the so-called "juggler" who was idealized in the 1980s. This was the have-it-all professional woman who pumped and froze breast milk before she whisked the baby off to day care and headed for the office, trim and smartly turned out with not a hair out of place, only to breeze home in the evening ready to slip into something comfortable and get in the mood for love. Well, at least that's what magazines and advertisements told us. In reality, nobody lived that way. We were guilt-racked and exhausted and self-effacing and absolutely sure that other women were succeeding where we were not. On the other hand, the real lives of most women have long been a miracle. Stretching small salaries; keeping children fed and clothed and carted to various activities; connecting family members, including in-laws; cooking and cleaning—women's lives are far from perfection, but they are perfectly amazing.

Still, there has to be a more just solution. So what would that be? Start by admitting to your daughter that you're not sure. What you do know is that for most women today, staying at home is not an option, both because they need to earn money and because they want to make a contribution in the world outside the home. You also know that what Debold, Wilson, and Malavé call the "girls will be boys" strategy, the Superwoman path, in which a woman takes on all the tasks and traits of a man while retaining all the tasks and traits of a woman, is unworkable.

Beyond that, there are new trends in which girls are declaring "girl power"—and as seductive as that sounds and as much as it seems to square with the focus on girls as strong and healthy, it too must be examined. This approach incorporates an "in your face" kind of sexuality and defiance, a "girls will be boys" type of action that assumes the world is less hostile than it really is. That kind of thinking in its extreme has been the genesis of the girl-gang phenomenon.

Given all this, how do you support your daughter's healthy desire to be a powerful, not-so-perfect girl? On a daily level, help your daughter give herself permission not to be perfect, not to be as thin as a supermodel, not to feel she has to sail through life with nary a misstep, not to think she's going to die of embarrassment when she trips, literally or figuratively. And on a grander scale, let her know that her generation has the power and the privilege of looking at what went wrong as well as what went right with the attempts previous generations made to find a way for women and men to fulfill their potential and collaborate successfully, both in the family and in the world at large. Finding a better way is the exciting challenge that faces our daughters as they head toward womanhood in the twenty-first century.

Activity: I Don't Have to Be Perfect

Have your daughter write an essay with her feelings on this topic. Tell her that it's OK if she refers to you and the fact that you are not perfect. Remind her once again, "If all we're ever told is to be good girls, how will we ever grow up to be great women?"

Resource:

Women, Girls, and Psychotherapy: Reframing Resistance, ed. by Carol Gilligan, Annie G. Rogers, and Deborah L. Tolman (Binghamton: Haworth Press, 1991).

52

An Ounce of Prevention Can Keep ALL Girls Strong

Number 9 lofted a fifteen-yard free kick that sailed over the defense and past the goalie to land smack in the upper left-hand corner of the net. The crowd went wild, and Number 9—an eight-year-old girl with obvious high self-esteem—grinned and raised both hands, fingers forming V signs. Her teammates did likewise. But the game, the final one of the season, wasn't over yet. With three minutes to go, the opposing jerseys had clearly resolved to do something about the fact that they were behind 2–1, with their dream of an undefeated season slipping away.

The girls displayed fierce determination, and when the clock showed little more than a minute left, three of the offensive players hurtled toward the goal. With seconds to go, one little Mia-Hamm-in-the-making connected with the ball and managed to get it across the plane of the goal line by the width of a fishing line. The referee signaled "Goal"! The girls were exultant. The parents were crying and cheering. Even the guy who sells hot dogs was crying and cheering. Surveying this, one father remarked wistfully, "If only our daughters could stay like this all their lives."

They can. We know that now. Girls don't have to slip into an emotional abyss at adolescence and then—if they're lucky—climb their way back out. Throughout this book, one of the problems we have addressed is finding ways to help older girls and women regain their self-esteem. But what is more important in the long run is to catch girls early enough so that we can *prevent* that loss of self-esteem in the first place. At the Ms. Foundation for Women, we have been working toward that end not only with Take Our Daughters to Work day but with many other projects, including the National Girls Initiative, the Collaborative Fund for Healthy Girls/Healthy Women, and the Girls, Young Women and Leadership program. Now, as the girls we have been reaching out to are hitting and going through puberty, we are beginning to see that our work has not been not in vain. The proverbial ounce of prevention appears to have been worth a pound of cure. Many of the girls who were seen and heard as children are proving to be more resilient and strong and sure of themselves in adolescence—and beyond.

We know that's what you want for all our daughters. The lessons in this book are meant to help you achieve on a personal level what we have done and are doing as a foundation. We hope you'll use the lessons to help not only your own daughter but—as the name Take Our Daughters to Work has always implied—all our nation's daughters.

Author and child advocate Neil Postman once wrote, "Children are living messages we send to a time we will never see." If we apply the lessons in this book to the lives of every girl whose life we can find a way to touch, our daughters will be able to dream of going where no girls have ever gone before. They will become living messages who will tell the world that we gave them what no generation of women ever had before: the realization that they can be full citizens of the world. Imagine a time when girls will move through adolescence and into womanhood with the same self-assured strides they took as children. Imagine a time when girls and women will always be seen and heard. Imagine a time when girls and women will be *safe* when they are seen and heard. Imagine a time when girls will grow up to take their rightful place alongside their brothers in every sphere now known to humankind and those yet to come. Imagine a time when that won't be remarkable but simply the way of the world.

We know that time will come. We have read the words of hundreds of girls who are already making a reality out of what we had only imagined. These girls are growing into adolescence with a more solid sense of self-esteem than even their older sisters had. The result is that they are less likely to lower their sights and may even raise them. They feel more entitled to full and rewarding lives, and many even believe they can become great women. Alexandra E. Desaulniers, a nine-year-old from Turner, Maine, is a fine example of this:

> **I** felt it shelter to speak to you.
>
> **Emily Dickinson**

During February school vacation this year, my mom and dad took me to Washington, D.C., for the first time. I went on a tour of the White House and saw paintings of all the Presidents. That's when I learned that there needs to be a change, because I learned that there has never been a woman President! I asked Mom about this, and she said that women can be President of the United States and that I can be President someday if I want to be.

I think that I would make a great President, so this year, I wrote to President Clinton asking him to let me go to work with him on Take Our Daughters to Work day. I haven't heard back yet, but I'll let you know when I do. Even if I can't go to work with him for the day, I'm still going to be President someday!

Whether or not Alexandra becomes the first female President of the United States—and with her clear-cut sense of direction, she just might—it's a safe bet that some girl from her cohort will. The surprise and indignation Alexandra registered when she saw all those paintings of male presidents is typical of a generation that is growing up with the expectation that women are capable of achieving and leading and making a difference. The women of the previous generation—those of us who are now mothering and mentoring the Alexandras of this world— were hamstrung by old mind-sets even as we struggled to break free and change the rules of the game so that we could be winners. Now there is every sign that our daughters are building emotional muscle so that they will stay strong in spirit and be trailblazers in the century to come—especially if we keep teaching them the life lessons that grew out of the lessons of one special day.

Alison Johnson, thirteen years old, has an idea for teaching those lessons to girls, now and in the years to come. Here is her account of how she came by her idea on Take Our Daughters to Work day:

First I went to my mother's work at the Department of Education. One of my best opportunities was appearing in a video public service announcement that was shown throughout the state of Florida. It was during this project that I began reading parts of Reviving Ophelia *that gave me a different point of view about being a preteen in middle school. It then gave me an idea. I can do a performance about* Reviving Ophelia. *I thought that putting* Reviving Ophelia *on stage would reach more middle school girls than the book. This is my dream, to work with Dr. Mary Pipher to put this on stage.*

Alison has no doubt that she can make that dream come true. And why not? As young as she is, she has already enjoyed a taste of success in the theater. In her words, "I landed the part of Helen Keller in *The Miracle Worker* for a production on Sanibel Island. In the newspapers, I was called a perfect role model for Women's History Month."

Winning the prize [1963 Nobel Prize in physics] wasn't half as exciting as doing the work itself.

Maria Goeppert Mayer

Alison and other girls like her are already making history. Imagine what the world will be like in the years to come if we never flag in our efforts to prevent girls from losing their self-esteem. After all, that loss would result in a huge cost to society because it would translate into a squandering of human potential. But when we give girls a place in the sun, when we take them to work on a day created for them alone, and when we make sure the effects of that one day are reinforced every day, we can keep our daughters confident that they can make the most of their potential, and make a difference as well. In the words of fifteen-year-old Crystal Burch of Aloha, Oregon, "I like this day because it is a window to the future."

And what a bright future that now promises to be.

Activity: I Could Go Down in History

Ask your daughter to imagine what she might do that would make history. She can write an essay and illustrate it for the final chapter in her book, I'M A GIRL WORTH WATCHING. Remember, however, that her book can keep growing as she grows, with new entries about new activities, new medals and citations, new information about what she is doing in the community, and new examples of ways she is working to change the world. Someday perhaps she'll share her book with a daughter of her own in a time when women in every walk of life will be where they are not because they had to break down barriers, but simply because women and men are people who do what they love and do it the very best they can.

Resource

National Women's History Project, 7738 Bell Road, Windsor, CA 95492-8518; 707-838-6000; fax 707-838-0478; (web site) http://www.nwho.org; (e-mail) nwhp@aol.com.

This is a not-for-profit educational organization that promotes women's rights through education about women's diverse lives and accomplishments. NWHP initiated National Women's History Month, now observed coast to coast every March.

Appendix

Reader's Guide

Circle of Strength

A Discussion and Action Guide
Based on the Lessons in This Book

Dear Reader,

What follows is a blueprint for putting into practice the principles we have discovered for making sure girls (and women) are seen and heard. You and your daughter can use this guide by yourselves, but experience has shown us that forming a circle of girls and women to share the adventure makes it immeasurably more valuable. Beyond that, the more diverse the membership, the richer the rewards and insights will be. For that reason, try to ensure that all generations are represented. The core of your circle will probably be mothers and their preadolescent or adolescent daughters, but in addition you can invite grandmothers, aunts, elderly neighbors, college students, young career women, young mothers, and empty nesters—either as regulars or as guests. Also, a multicultural mix of members helps expand everyone's thinking.

Because you want to encourage openness and intimacy, you're best off keeping the number of members to no more than fifteen or twenty. If there are more people who want to join, why not form a second or third group? Perhaps all the groups could plan to get together once or twice a year.

You may want to hold your meetings in members' homes, or you may choose to use a facility such as a community center, the library, or the basement of a house of worship. Plan on about an hour for each session. Meetings may be held weekly, biweekly, or monthly, depending on members' schedules. Getting together any less frequently than that, though, tends to cause interest to flag, and the group may end up disbanding.

She's the One!

Obviously, as is true in any organization, someone needs to be at the helm. You may either appoint or elect a person to coordinate schedules, address lists, and phone chains. The coordinator could preside for a specified term, perhaps six months or a year, before someone else takes over the responsibilities.

However, each member will benefit from having a turn at being the leader at a meeting. The group will also benefit from a system that allows each member to be seen and heard. Some mother/daughter pairs may choose to co-lead. The designated coordinator can keep track of the leader rotation.

To begin each session, the leader of the day might like to share something unique about her lifestyle or heritage—ethnic food, music and customs, or recommendations of books and activities she's found useful and fun within her own family.

Consider Yourself One of Us!

If a new member is being welcomed into the circle or if a guest has been invited, the leader of the day will want to introduce the inductee or guest at the beginning of the meeting. This is a good time to review any ground rules you may have established, such as an agreement that personal stories shared within the group will be kept confidential, and an explanation of the rotating leadership system.

Clasping Hands

The first order of business after the leader's welcome and introductions can be a literal circle of strength, with members holding hands all around. If you develop a motto or ritual greeting, you can recite it together at this point. However, simply standing in silence for a moment is also a powerful method of establishing a trusting connection with one another.

Speaking in the Spotlight

Next, the leader of the day gets her chance to be seen and heard. This is a time for her to share a story or an insight, a triumph or a challenge, a life-changing event or a new sense of direction. Photographs, citations, medals, and other kudos can be part of the presentation. Anything from a fifth-grader letting everyone know she won a swim meet to an older woman announcing the birth of her first grandchild to a midlife woman celebrating a promotion at work qualifies.

If this smacks of that kindergarten staple "show and tell," that's because there is an intentional similarity. Being seen and heard, standing up and speaking positively about oneself, letting others know about one's own accomplishments and strengths—these behaviors need not be the domain of the very young. Throughout their lives, girls and women need opportunities to be in the spotlight and to validate themselves publicly. Try to overcome any culturally induced reticence and embarrassment you may have acquired over the years, and see whether you can find in yourself that eager little girl who once clamored unselfconsciously for a turn to be seen and heard.

Cheers and Jeers

Invite members to be on the alert for both positive and negative examples in the media regarding gender roles and stereotyping. People can bring in actual newspaper and magazine ads and articles, and also mention television and radio spots, movies, and billboards. As your group meetings continue and you begin to work on some of the activities in this guide, you may have the satisfaction of seeing the results of your own letter-writing campaign to a particular manufacturer or publisher.

Great Girls/Great Women

This is the portion of the meeting when members can mention any notable progress by girls and women, both in the local community and in the world at large. Newspaper and magazine clippings about events such as the election of a female mayor or the establishment of a girls' athletic association at the high school can be used to illustrate the achievements.

Life Lesson

By now about half an hour will probably have elapsed, and you're ready to devote the remaining meeting time to a main theme. We have prepared suggestions for using the chapters in this book as jumping-off points for discussions, writing exercises, and activities. (A chalkboard or an easel with a large pad of paper is useful for writing the day's theme and any key discussion questions.) The sequence we have chosen moves from the personal (retaining and regaining self-esteem) to the practical (education and work) to society at large (effecting change for the better). Feel free, however, to adapt the guidelines to suit the needs of your group. You may also want to go back to certain sections over time as new needs arise or new insights occur to you.

I. Ready, Set, Grow!

Each of the eighteen chapters in Part One of this book is devoted to an aspect of the process of self-discovery, as well as an exploration of the ways in which girls and women can make sure their true selves continue to evolve over a lifetime. At the first meeting dedicated to Part One, the leader of the day can pose the following discussion question: *How do I nurture my nature?*

Encourage members to talk about the concept of one's "nature" (inborn qualities, talents, and predilections) and "nurture" (how a person is affected by the way she is brought up and by the society around her). Consider the fact that the seventeenth-century philosopher John Locke put forth a theory that at birth each of us is a *tabula rasa*, or "clean slate." Do members agree or disagree? What about the East Indian philosophy of the "dharma," which holds that each person is born with a unique constellation of gifts and a special potential that should be developed? (See Chapter 8.) Do members agree or disagree?

The leader of the day should guide the discussion using the technique described in Chapter 2. Also, a member with a dissenting opinion should validate what another person has said by beginning with a sentence such as, "That's an interesting point you made, but I'd like to look at it another way." When people are speaking their minds and allowing concepts to form, no one is "right" or "wrong." There is also no need to arrive at a consensus. The goal is to stimulate further thought, air ideas, and perhaps continue the discussion at a future meeting when members have had a chance to ruminate a bit.

As a *writing exercise,* members can take home the question, "How do I nurture my nature?" and explore the answers in their personal journals. The corollary, of course, is, "How am I failing to nurture my nature?" The result of the writing might be an *action:* a resolution and a plan to rectify a situation in which a girl or woman has been denying her true self and her needs.

At subsequent meetings dedicated to Part One of this book, use each chapter heading in turn as the starting point of your *discussion.* The chapters are concise enough that members can read one in preparation for each meeting. If a particular chapter is augmented by a quote from a notable woman, include that quote as a point of *discussion.* After each meeting, *writing* one's reactions to the discussion will solidify the experience and perhaps bring up new questions, either personal ones to be pondered or more public ones to be shared at the next meeting.

Also, note that at the end of each chapter, there are related resources such as books for further reading, videos, and web sites. The leader of the day might like to act as a reviewer of these resources. If she obtains a copy of a recommended book that she feels is particularly useful, she could circulate it among members with a library-style borrowers' list. If a particular video would benefit the whole group, she could use some of the meeting time for viewing and a follow-up discussion, or request a special meeting solely for this purpose. Similarly, if a web site is especially interesting, perhaps a member with access to the Internet could host a meeting so that everyone could visit the site. Alternately, the group may be able to locate a public computer, perhaps at an Internet cafe or in the school resource room.

II. Learning and Earning

The fourteen chapters in Part Two of this book deal with education, both formal and informal, as well as work options. A key component of this section is the importance of a mentor. For the first meeting dedicated to this portion of the book, members should read Chapter 19 and be prepared for a *discussion* guided by the following questions:

1) Who is (was) your mentor?
2) How does (did) your mentor help and inspire you?
3) Are you a mentor?
4) If so, how do you help and inspire your mentee?
5) Is mentoring a mutually beneficial process? That is, does the mentor not only give to the mentee but receive from her as well? Why or why not?

At subsequent meetings, you may want to invite members' mentors as guest speakers. Also, as with Part One, it's a good idea to devote one meeting to each chapter, and you may want to invite guests whose expertise or area of interest correlates with a particular chapter's theme. For example, for Chapter 20, invite women who are following nontraditional careers. For Chapter 21, invite women who have successfully pursued two or more career paths, either simultaneously or in sequence. For Chapter 25, invite a girl or young woman who is a successful entrepreneur. For Chapter 26, invite a father who wants to share his experiences with raising a daughter. For Chapter 27, invite a teacher or a principal. For Chapter 28, invite a woman who is an accomplished mathematician and a woman who is a scientist. Also for Chapter 28, encourage adult members to talk about how they have used math and science in their work and their lives in general. For Chapter 29, invite a woman who is a web site designer or computer programmer. These are merely suggestions, of course. Brainstorm with your group about other possibilities.

Again, the leader of the day can be the reviewer for the materials listed at the end of the chapter she is responsible for. And throughout the weeks when Part Two is being read and discussed, recommend *writing* about each topic (for example, an exploration of why a mentor is important) and then taking *action* if necessary or possible (writing a letter to a potential mentor).

After finishing Chapter 32, and before moving on to Part Three, hold a special meeting devoted to the theme of staying in school. As a *discussion*, have members of all ages respond to the following:

1) What I like(d) about school
2) What I hate(d) about school

Be absolutely honest. You may find some striking similarities in your feelings. Do a majority of members complain that boys get more attention than girls? Are a lot of members upset because history books largely ignore women? Do many members feel that guidance counselors are not effective enough in encouraging girls to prepare for non-traditional careers? If you see a pattern, why not resolve to take *action*? As a group, draft a letter to the local school board and administration expressing your views and offering suggestions for changes and improvements. If you get a response, follow up by inviting a key person to one of your meetings. Educators have exactly the same goals you have: providing a quality education for all students and keeping students in school. Enlist educators as allies for making sure those goals are reached.

III. Making a Difference

Part Three of this book has to do with learning to voice opinions and take *action*, both as individuals and as part of a group. If you followed the suggestion in the previous section to work together to effect changes in your schools, you already know that there is strength in numbers. Now, take that knowledge with you into the final phase of working through this book together.

As you have been doing all along, devote one meeting to each of the remaining twenty chapters, using the title as a spur for *discussion* and follow-up *writing*, and having each leader in turn act as a reviewer for the resources for her chapter. However, when you get to chapters which involve learning to identify causes and organizing to make a difference, plan to spend the last ten or fifteen minutes of each meeting taking concrete steps toward reaching joint goals. For Chapter 37, you might want to find out how to organize a "Take Back the Night" rally. For Chapter 38, your group may decide to enroll in self-defense courses together. For Chapters 39 and 40, why not take on the media and write letters suggesting changes in ads, articles, shows, and broadcasts that you find offensive or that promote gender stereotyping? For Chapter 46, you could get a campaign going for equal pay for equal work. And for Chapter 49, find a cause you believe in—Meals on Wheels, a local shelter for runaway teens, or a literacy program for midlife women—and work as a group to put your beliefs into *action*.

Beyond volunteering time and talents, however, consider giving money to support your causes. Martha Taylor, a founder of the Women's Philanthropy Institute in Madison, Wisconsin, is quoted as saying that women "need to learn how to influence society with their gifts. Men have generally been active philanthropists, not shy in telling organizations what their values are and what they want done with a gift."

The Ms. Foundation for Women found that women want to leverage their money by giving together and learning about the issues they fund. One way to accomplish this is simply to earmark certain funds for phil-anthropic purposes. Your group could adapt a concept put into practice by the Milwaukee Women's Fund. They set up the "Little Women's Fund," which seeks gifts of $1,000 or more to be made in the name of a female baby. From the time the girl is five until she reaches adulthood, the fund will send her educational materials about how to give wisely, volunteer, and manage her money. When she reaches her thirties, she will be encouraged to direct the money in her fund to her favorite causes.

Looking at this model, your group could accept contributions from members—say, $25 each—and put the money in an interest-bearing account specifically designated to advance an agreed-upon cause or help a certain charity. If you have twenty members, your fund would have $500 to begin with. The interest will keep it growing, and you can also choose to add to it through old-fashioned fund-raising (car washes, garage sales, raffles). When you eventually give the money to a not-for-profit charitable organization, members can deduct the original $25 gift to the extent allowable by law.

When your group reaches the point where you have covered all fifty-two chapters in this book, you will have put into motion many activities that will keep you going strong for as long as you like. The resource lists alone constitute a nearly inexhaustible reservoir of information, and can serve to spark potential *discussions, writing exercises,* and *actions.* Also, the web sites will constantly be updated, supplying you with fresh material for meetings. Then, too, the volunteer work and philanthropy that you have begun can go on indefinitely. You may also wish to return to various chapters of this book for refresher sessions, and you can always look for new guest speakers to broaden your awareness and interests and guide you toward new ventures, both personally and as a group interested in social change.

Until We Meet Again

At the close of each meeting, regroup and clasp hands once more in your circle of strength. Repeat your motto and/or stand in silence for a moment. Then release hands and mingle as you say your good-byes. You can shake hands, embrace, congratulate one another, thank one another, mention what you liked most about the meeting—whatever you feel genuinely moved to do as a result of the connection you feel because of the work you are doing to improve your own lives and the lives of all girls and women.

———

We welcome your feedback. Did reading *Girls Seen and Heard* encourage you to make changes in your life and the life of your daughter? Are you members of a Circle of Strength? If so, how has the group experience affected you and your daughter thus far? Did you find the guidelines for forming a circle to be useful? Do you have any suggestions for further guidelines, based on the way your group has evolved?

We would also like to hear your stories. Tell us about any successes you and your group have had in making a difference both in your own lives and in the culture we live in.

Send letters to "Girls Seen and Heard," c/o Ms. Foundation for Women, 120 Wall Street, 33rd Floor, New York, NY 10005.

We look forward to your input. May all of us and all of our daughters always be seen and heard.

Sincerely,

The Ms. Foundation for Women

Resources

Organizations

AAUW (American Association of University Women); 1111 16th Street, NW, Washington, D.C. 20036; 202-785-7700; TDD 202-785-7777; fax 202-872-1425; (web site) http://www.aauw.org; (e-mail) info@mail.aauw.org.

AIDS and Adolescents Network of New York; 666 Broadway, Suite 5201, New York, NY 10012; 212-505-9115; fax 212-505-2668.

Advocates for Youth; 1025 Vermont Ave., NW, Suite 200, Washington, D.C. 20005; 202-347-5700; (web site) http://www.advocatesfory-outh.org; (e-mail) info@advocatesforyouth.org.

AFL-CIO; 815 16th St., NW, Washington, D.C. 20006; 202-637-5000; fax 202-637-5058; (web site) http://www.aflcio.org.

After School Action Programs; 1126 West Granville, Chicago, IL 60660; 773-973-0158; fax 773-973-0578.

Alanon-Alateen Family Groups; 1600 Corporate Landing Parkway, Virginia Beach, VA 23454; 800-356-9996; (web site) http://www.al-anon-alateen.org; (e-mail) info@al-anon-alateen.org.

Alpha Kappa Alpha Sorority; 5656 South Stoney Island Ave., Chicago, IL 60637; 773-684-1282; fax 773-288-8251; (web site) http://www.aka.1908.com.

American Anorexia/Bulimia Association; 165 West 46th St., Suite 1108, New York, NY 10036; 212-575-6200; (web site) http://members.aol.com/amanbu; (e-mail) amanbu@aol.com.

American Civil Liberties Union, Lesbian and Gay Rights Project; 125 Broad St., New York, NY 10004-2440; 212-944-9800; fax 212-869-9061; (web site) http://www.aclu.org.

American Council of the Blind; 1155 15th St., NW, Suite 720, Washington, D.C. 20005; 202-467-5081; fax 202-467-5085; (web site) http://acb.org.

American Women's Self-Defense Association; 713 N. Wellwood Ave., Lindenhurst, NY 11757; 516-226-8383; 800-43-AWSDA (800-432-9732); fax 516-226-5454; (web site) http://www.awsda.org; (e-mail) awsda@nais.com.

An Income of Her Own; 1804 W. Burbank Blvd., Burbank, CA 91506; 800-350-1816; (web site) http://www.anincomeofherown.com.

The ARC; 500 E. Border St., Suite 300, Arlington, TX 76010; 817-261-6003; TDD 817-277-0553; fax 817-277-3491; (web site) http://www.thearc.org; (e-mail) thearc@metronet.com.

Asian and Pacific Environmental Network; 310 8th St., Suite 309, Oakland, CA 94607; 510-834-8920; fax 510-834-8926; (e-mail) apen@igc.apc.org.

Asians and Pacific Islanders for Reproductive Health; 12377 Lewis St., Suite 205, Garden Grove, CA 92840; 213-694-3539; fax 213-664-7393; (e-mail) apirh@igc.org.

Aspira; 1444 I St., NW, Suite 800, Washington, D.C. 20005; 202-835-3600; fax 202-835-3613; (web site) http://www.incacorp.com/aspira; (e-mail) aspira1@aol.com.

BAMM/Impact Self-Defense; 629 Bair Island Rd., Suite 104, Redwood, CA 94063; 800-345-KICK; (web site) http://www.bamm.org; (e-mail) info@bamm.org.

Big Brothers/Big Sisters of America; 230 N. 13th St., Philadelphia, PA 19107; 215-567-7000; fax 215-567-0394; (web site) http://www.bbbsa.org; (e-mail) bbbsa@aol.com.

Boys and Girls Clubs; 771 First Ave., New York, NY 10017-3506; 212-351-5480; fax 212-351-5493; (web site) http://www.bgca.org.

Campaign for Tobacco-Free Kids; 1707 L St., NW, Washington, D.C. 20036; 800-284-KIDS; fax 202-296-5427; (web site) http://www.toboaccofreekids.org.

Camp Fire Boys and Girls; 4601 Madison Ave., Kansas City, MO 64112; 816-756-1950; fax 816-756-0258; (web site) http://www.campfire.org (e-mail) info@campfire.org.

Catalyst; 120 Wall St., 5th Floor, New York, NY 10005; 212-514-7600; fax 212-514-8470.

Center for Anti-Violence Education; 421 Fifth Ave., Brooklyn, NY 11215; 718-788-1775; fax 718-369-3192.

Center for Young Women's Development; 1095 Market St., #608, San Francisco, CA 94103; 415-487-8662; fax 415-487-8665; (e-mail) cfyw@igc.apc.org.

Children Now; 1212 Broadway, Suite 530, Oakland, CA 94612; 510-763-2444; fax 510-763-1974; (web site) http://www.childrennow.org; (e-mail) children@dnai.com.

Children's Defense Fund; 25 E Street, NW, Washington, D.C. 20001; 202-628-8787; fax 202-662-3510; (web site) http://www.childrendefense.org; (e-mail) edfinfo@childrendefense.org.

Coalition of Labor Union Women; 1126 16th St., NW, Room 104, Washington, D.C. 20036; 202-466-4615; fax 202-776-0537.

Cool Girls; 100 Edgewood Ave., NE #508, Atlanta, GA 30303; 404-420-4362; fax 404-420-4366.

Delta Sigma Theta; 1707 New Hampshire Ave., NW, Washington, D.C. 20009; 202-986-2400; fax 202-986-2513; (web site) http://www.dst1913.org.

Disability Rights Education and Defense Fund; 2212 Sixth St., Berkeley, CA 94710; 510-644-2555, TDD: 510-644-2626; 800-466-4232 (ADA hot line, voice, and TDD); fax 510-841-6812; (e-mail) dredf@dredf.org.

Eating Disorders Awareness and Prevention; 603 Stewart St., Suite 803, Seattle, WA 98101; 206-382-3587; fax 206-292-9890; (web site) http://members.aol.com/edapinc.

The Entrepreneurial Development Institute (TEDI); 2025 I Street, NW, Washington, D.C. 20006; 202-822-8334; fax 202-822-5090.

The Fatherhood Project; 330 7th Ave., 14th Floor, New York, NY 10001; 212-465-2044; fax 212-465-8637; (web site) http://www.familiesandwork.org.

Families and Work Institute; 330 7th Ave., 14th Floor, New York, NY 10001; 212-465-2044; fax 212-465-8637; (web site) http://www.familiesandwork.org.

Feminist Majority; 1600 Wilson Blvd., Suite 801, Arlington, VA 22209; 703-522-2214; fax 703-522-2219; (web site) http://www.feminist.org; (e-mail) femmaj@feminist.org.

Girl Games; 221 E. 9th St., Suite 302, Austin, TX 78701; 888-GRLS-RUL (888-475-7785); (web site) http://www.planetgirl.com; (e-mail) info@girlgamesinc.com.

Girl Power!; U.S. Department of Health and Human Service Center for Substance Abuse, 11426 Rockville Pike, Suite 100, Rockville, MD 20852; 800-729-6686; TDD 800-487-4889; (web site) http://www.health.org/gpower.

Girls Count, 225 E. 16th Ave., Suite 475, Denver, CO 80203; 303-832-6600; fax 303-832-7331; (web site) http://www.girlscount.org; (e-mail) gc@girlscount.org.

Girl Scouts of the USA, 420 Fifth Ave., New York, NY 10018, 212-852-8000; fax 212-852-6512; (web site) http://www.gsusa.org; (e-mail) admin@www.gsusa.org.

Girls Incorporated; 120 Wall St., New York, NY 10004; 212-689-3700; fax 212-683-1253; National Resource Center; 441 W. Michigan St., Indianapolis, IN, 46202-3235; (web site) http://www.girlsinc.org; (e-mail) hn3580@handsnet.org.

Girls International Forum; 2127 Columbus Ave., Duluth, MN 55803; 218-728-5507; fax 218-728-0314; (e-mail) newmoon@newmoon.duluth.mn.us.org.

Hetrick-Martin Institute; 2 Astor Place, New York, NY 10003; 212-674-2400; TTY 212-674-8695; fax 212-674-8650; (e-mail) hmi@hmi.org.

Indian Youth of America; 609 Badgerow Building, P.O. Box 2786, Sioux City, Iowa 51106; 712-252-3230; fax 712-252-3712.

MANA, A National Latina Organization; 1725 K St., NW, Suite 501, Washington, D.C. 20006; 202-833-0060; fax 202-496-0588; (web site) http://www.hermana.org; (e-mail) hermana@aol.com.

Marymount Institute for the Education of Women and Girls (*The Equity Newsletter*); Marymount Ave., Tarrytown, NY 10591-3796; 914-332-4917.

Mentors in Violence Prevention/MVP Project; Northeastern University's Center for the Study of Sport in Society; 360 Huntington Ave., Suite 161 CP, Boston, MA 02115; 617-373-4025; fax 617-373-4566; (web site) http://www.sportinsociety.org.

Mi Casa Resource Center for Women; 571 Galapago St., Denver, CO 80204; 303-573-1302; fax 303-595-0422; (e-mail) micasa@sni.net.

Myra Sadker Advocates for Gender Equity; Suite 300, 1401 Rockville Pike, Rockville, MD 20852; 301-738-7113; fax 301-424-0474; (e-mail) Dsadker@aol.com.

National Association of Women Business Owners; 1100 Wayne Ave., Suite 830, Silver Spring, MD 20910; 301-608-2590; fax 301-608-2596; (web site) http://www.nawbo.org; (e-mail) nawbohq@aol.com.

National Black Child Development Institute; 1023 15th St., NW, Suite 600, Washington, D.C. 20005; 202-387-1281; fax 202-234-1738; (web site) http://www.nbcdi.org; (e-mail) moreinfo@nbcdi.org.

National Black Women's Health Project; 1211 Connecticut Ave., NW, Suite 310; Washington, D.C. 20005; 202-835-0117; fax 202-833-8790; (e-mail) nbwhpdc@aol.com.

National Center for Youth with Disabilities (NCYD); University of Minnesota, Adolescent Health Program, Box 721, 420 Delaware St., SE, Minneapolis, MN 55455; 612-626-2825.

National Clearinghouse for Alcohol and Drug Information; U.S. Department of Health and Human Service Center for Substance Abuse, 11426 Rockville Pike, Suite 100, Rockville, MD 20852; 800-729-6686; (web site) http://www.health.org/gpower.

National Clearinghouse for Women and Girls with Disabilities Education Equity Concepts; 114 East 32nd Street, Suite 701, New York, NY 10016; 212-725-1803 (voice/TTY); fax 212-725-0947; (web site) http://www.onisland.com/eec; (e-mail) 75507.1306@compuserve.com.

National Coalition of Girls' Schools; 228 Main St., Concord, MA 01742; 508-287-4485; fax 508-287-6014; (web site) http://www.ncgs.org; (e-mail) ncgs@ncgs.org.

National Coalition of 100 Black Women; 38 West 32nd St., Suite 1610, New York, NY 10001; 212-947-2196; fax 212-947-2477; (web site) http://www.womenconnect.com/ncbw; (e-mail) nc100bw@aol.com.

National Council of La Raza; 1111 19th St., NW, Suite 1000, Washington, D.C. 20036; 202-785-1670; fax 202-776-1792; (web site) http://www.nclr.org.

National Information Center for Children and Youth with Disabilities; P.O. Box 1492, Washington, D.C. 20013; 202-884-8200; TDD 800-695-0285; fax 202-884-8441; (web site) http://www.nichcy.org; (e-mail) nichcy@aed.org.

National Organization on Disability; 910 16th St., NW, Suite 600; Washington, D.C. 20006; 202-293-5960; TDD: 202-293-5968; fax 202-293-7999; (web site) http://www.nod.org; (e-mail) ability@nod.org.

National Organization for Women (NOW); 1000 16th St., NW, Suite 700, Washington, D.C. 20036; 202-331-0066; fax 202-785-8576; (web site) http://www.now.org; (e-mail) now@now.org.

National Rehabilitation Information Center; 8455 Colesville Rd., Suite 935, Silver Spring, MD 20910; 800-346-2742; TTY 301-495-5626; fax 301-587-1967; (web site) http://www.naric.com/naric.

National Urban League; 120 Wall St., 8th Floor, New York, NY 10005; 212-558-5300; fax 212-558-5332; (web site) http://www.nul.org; (e-mail) info@nul.org.

National Women's History Project; 7738 Bell Rd., Windsor, CA 95492-8518; 707-838-6000; fax 707-838-0478; (web site) http://www.nwhp.org; (e-mail) nwhp@aol.com.

Native Action; P.O. Box 409, Lame Deer, MT 59043; 406-477-6390; fax 406-477-6421; (e-mail) gsmall@mcn.com.

9to5, National Association of Working Women, 238 W. Wisconsin Ave., Suite 700, Milwaukee, WI 53203-2308, 414-274-0925; fax 414-272-2870.

Oakland Men's Project; 1203 Preservation Park Way, #200, Oakland, CA 94612; 510-835-2433; fax 510-835-2466.

Planned Parenthood Federation of America, 810 7th Ave., New York, NY 10019; 212-541-7800; 800-829-7732; fax 212-245-1845; (web site) http://www.plannedparenthood.org.

Research for Action (RFA), International House, 3701 Chestnut St., Suite 6W, Philadelphia, PA 19104; 215-823-2500; fax 215-823-2510.

Sexuality Information and Education Council of the United States (SIECUS); 130 W. 42nd St., Suite 350, New York, NY 10036-7802; 212-819-9770; (web site) http://www.siecus.org; (e-mail) siecus@siecus.org.

Sigma Gamma Rho Sorority; 8800 Stony Island Ave., Chicago, IL 60617; 773-873-9000; fax 773-731-9642.

Sisters in Portland Impacting Real Action Together; 5806 North Albina, Portland, OR 97217; 503-283-5340; fax 503-283-1289; (e-mail) massaction@igc.apc.org.

A Sporting Chance Foundation; 1940 W. Irving Park Rd., Suite No. 2, Chicago, IL 60613; 773-935-2401; fax 773-935-2420.

Stand for Children; 1834 Connecticut Avenue, NW, Washington, D.C. 20009; 202-234-0095; fax 202-234-0391; (web site) http://www.stand.org; (e-mail) stand@stand.org.

Step by Step; 659 Big Ugly Creek Rd. East, Harts, WV 25524; 304-855-8557; fax 304-855-5050; (e-mail) SBS@wnpb.wnet.edu.

U.S. Department of Labor, Women's Bureau; 200 Constitution Avenue, NW, Room S-3002, Washington, D.C. 20210; 202-219-6593; (web site) http://www.dol.gov/dol/wb.

White Buffalo Calf Women Society; P.O. Box 227, Mission, SD 57555-0227; 605-856-2317; fax 605-856-2994.

Women's College Coalition and the Ad Council (Expect the Best from a Girl, That's What You'll Get); 125 Michigan Ave., NE, Washington, D.C. 20017; 202-234-0443; 800-WCC4GIRLS; (web site) http://www.academic.org.

Women's Education Equity Act (WEEA) Resource Center, Education Development Center, Inc.; 800-225-3088 and 800-793-5076; (web site) http://www.edc.org/womensequity.

Women's Sports Foundation; Eisenhower Park; East Meadow, NY 11554; 516-542-4700; 800-227-3988; fax 516-542-4716; (web site) http://www.lifetimetv.com/WoSport; (e-mail) WoSporttbs@aol.com.

YMCA of the USA; 101 North Wacker Dr., 14th Floor, Chicago, IL 60606; 1-800-872-9622; fax 312-977-9063; (web site) http://www.ymca.net.

YWCA, Empire State Building, 350 Fifth Ave., Suite 301, New York, NY 10118; 212-273-7800; fax 212-465-2281; (web site) http://www.ywca.org.

Young Women's Project; 923 F St., NW, 3rd Floor, Washington, D.C. 20004; 202-393-0461; fax 202-393-0065.

Zeta Phi Beta Sorority; 1734 New Hampshire Ave., NW, Washington, D.C. 20009; 202-387-3103; fax 202-232-4593; (web site) http://www.zpb1920.org.

Books and Other Publications

The AAUW Report: How Schools Shortchange Girls, The AAUW Educational Foundation and National Educational Association, Washington, D.C. 1992.

All That She Can Be: Helping Your Daughter Maintain Her Self-Esteem, Dr. Carol Eagle and Carol Colman; Simon & Schuster, New York, 1993.

Altered Loves: Mothers and Daughters During Adolescence, Terri Apter; St. Martin's, New York, 1990.

Am I Thin Enough Yet?, Sharlene Hesse-Biber; Oxford University Press, New York, 1995.

Anatomy of Love, Helen Fisher; Norton, New York, 1992.

The Beauty Myth: How Images of Beauty Are Used Against Women, Naomi Wolf; William Morrow, New York, 1991.

Best Friends and Marriage: Exchange Among Women, Stacey Oliker; University of California Press, Berkeley, CA, 1989.

Beyond Dolls and Guns: 101 Ways to Help Children Avoid Gender Bias, Susan Hoy Crawford; Heinemann, Portsmouth, NH, 1995.

The Body Project, Joan Jacobs Brumberg; Random House, New York, 1997.

Boiling Point, Kevin Phillips; Random House, New York, 1993.

Boys Will Be Boys: Breaking the Link Between Masculinity and Violence, Myriam Miedzian; Doubleday, New York, 1991.

Celebrating Girls: Nurturing and Empowering Our Daughters, Virginia Beane Rutter; Conari Press, Berkeley, CA, 1996.

Choices: A Teen Woman's Journal for Self-Awareness and Personal Planning, Mindy Bingham, Judy Edmondson, and Sandy Stryker, Advocacy Press, Santa Barbara, CA, 1985 (updated 1993).

Dating Violence: Young Women in Danger, Barrie Levy, ed.; Seal Press, Seattle, 1991.

The Difference: Growing Up Female in America, Judy Mann; Warner Books, New York, 1994.

Don't Stop Loving Me: A Reassuring Guide for Mothers of Adolescent Daughters, Ann F. Carson; Harperperennial, New York, 1992.

Emotional Intelligence, Daniel Goleman; Bantam Books, New York, 1995.

Failing at Fairness: How Our Schools Cheat Girls, Myra and David Sadker; Touchstone Books, New York, 1995.

Family Politics: Love and Power on an Intimate Frontier, Letty Cottin Pogrebin; McGraw-Hill, New York, 1984.

Femininity, Susan Brownmiller; Fawcett, New York, 1985.

The First Time, Karen Bouris; Conari Press, Berkeley, CA, 1994.

For All Our Daughters, Pegine Echevarria; Chandler House Press, Worcester, MA, 1998.

Free to Be . . . You and Me, Carol Hart, Letty Cottin Pogrebin, Mary Rodgers, and Marlo Thomas eds.; McGraw-Hill, New York, 1998.

Get a Financial Life: Personal Finance in Your Twenties and Thirties, Beth Kobliner; Fireside, New York, 1996.

Get Smart: What You Should Know (But Won't Learn in Class) About Sexual Harassment and Sex Discrimination (2nd edition), Montana Katz and Veronica Vieland; The Feminist Press at CUNY, New York, 1993.

Girl Talk: Staying Strong, Feeling Good, Sticking Together, Judith Harlan; Walker, New York, 1997.

The Girl Within, Emily Hancock; Ballantine Books, New York, 1990.

GirlPower: Young Women Speak Out, Hillary Carlip; Warner Books, New York, 1995.

Girls and Young Women Leading the Way: 20 True Stories About Leadership, Frances A. Karnes and Suzanne M. Bea; Free Spirit Publishing, Minneapolis, 1993.

The Girls' Guide to Life: How to Take Charge of the Issues That Affect You, Catherine Dee; Little, Brown, Boston, 1997.

Girls in the Middle: Working to Succeed in School, Jody Cohen and Sukey Blanc; Research for Action, the AAUW Educational Foundation, Washington, D.C., 1996.

Girls Know Best: Written by Girls Just Like You, compiled by Michelle Roehm; Beyond Words Publishing, Hillsboro, OR, 1997.

Girls Speak Out, Andrea Johnson; Scholastic, New York, 1997.

Girls to the Rescue, Bruce Lansky; Meadowbrook Press, Minnetonka, MN, 1995.

Going for the Gold: Shannon Miller, Septima Green; Avon, New York, 1996.

Great Books for Girls, Kathleen Odean; Ballantine Books, New York, 1997.

Growing a Girl: Seven Strategies for Raising a Strong, Spirited Daughter, Dr. Barbara Mackoff; Dell Publishers, New York, 1996.

Healthy Divorce, Craig Everett and Sandra V. Everett, Jossey Bass Publishers, San Francisco, 1994.

Helping Teens Stop Violence: A Practical Guide for Counselors, Educators and Parents, Allan Creighton and Paul Kivel; Hunter House, Alameda, CA, 1992.

Herstory: Women Who Changed the World, Ruth Ashby and Deborah Gore Ohrn eds.; Viking, New York, 1995.

Hostile Hallways, the AAUW Educational Foundation; research by Harris Scholastic Research, Washington, D.C., 1993.

How to Father a Successful Daughter, Nicky Marone; Ballantine, New York, 1988.

I Am Beautiful: A Celebration of Women in Their Own Words, Dana Carpenter and Woody Winfree eds.; Rose Communications, Berkeley, CA, 1997.

It's a Girl Thing: How to Stay Healthy, Safe, and in Charge, Mavis Jukes; Knopf, New York, 1996.

It Takes a Village: And Other Lessons Children Teach Us, Hillary Rodham Clinton; Touchstone Books, New York, 1996.

Jackie Joyner-Kersee: Champion Athlete, Geri Harrington; Chelsea House, New York, 1995.

Let's Talk About Me: A Girl's Personal, Private and Portable Instruction Book for Life, from Girl Games; Archway, New York, 1997.

Let's Talk About Me: The Girl's Interactive Handbook for the 21st Century (CD-ROM); Simon and Schuster Interactive, New York, 1996.

Mad at Miles: A Blackwoman's Guide to Truth, Pearl Cleage; Cleage Group, Southfield, MI, 1990.

Meeting at the Crossroads, Lyn Mikel Brown and Carol Gilligan; Ballantine Books, New York, 1992.

The Mother-Daughter Book Club, Shireen Dodson; HarperCollins, New York, 1997.

Mother Daughter Revolution: From Good Girls to Great Women, Elizabeth DeBold, Marie Wilson, and Idelisse Malavé; Bantam, New York, 1994.

The Neuter Computer: Computers for Girls and Boys, Jo Sanders and Antonia Stone; Neal-Schuman Publishers, New York, 1986.

No More Frogs to Kiss: 99 Ways to Give Economic Power to Girls, Jolene Godfrey; HarperCollins, New York, 1995.

Out of Work: A History of Wage-Earning Women in the United States, Alice Kessler-Harris; Oxford University Press, New York, 1982.

The Parents' Book About Divorce, Richard Gardener; Bantam Books, New York, 1991.

A Parent's Guide for Suicidal and Depressed Teens: Help for Recognizing if a Child is in Crisis and What to Do About It, Kate Williams; Hazeldon Foundation, Center City, MN, 1995.

Peace Is Every Step: The Path of Mindfulness in Everyday Life, Thich Nhat Hanh; Ballantine Books, New York, 1992.

The Period Book: Everything You Don't Want to Ask (But Need to Know), Karen Gravelle and Jennifer Gravelle; Walker, New York, 1996.

Powerplays: How Teens Can Pull the Plug on Sexual Harassment, Harriet Hodgson; Fairview Press, Minneapolis, 1996.

Reflections of Risk: Growing Up Female in Minnesota, Minnesota Women's Fund, Minneapolis, February 1990.

Reviving Ophelia: Saving the Selves of Adolescent Girls, Mary Pipher; Ballantine Books, New York, 1994.

Revolution from Within, Gloria Steinem; Little Brown, Boston, 1992.

SchoolGirls: Young Women, Self-Esteem and the Confidence Gap, Peggy Orenstein; Doubleday, New York, 1994.

Screen Smarts: A Family Guide to Media Literacy, Gloria DeGaetano and Kathleen Bander; Houghton Mifflin Company, New York, 1996.

The Second Shift: Working Parents and the Revolution at Home, Arlie Hoschschild; Viking, New York, 1989.

Secrets in Public: Sexual Harassment in Our Schools, Nan Stein, Nancy Marshall, and Linda Tropp; the NOW Legal Defense and Education Fund and the Wellesley College Center for Research on Women, Wellesley, MA, 1993.

Sexual Harassment: High School Girls Speak Out, June Larkin; Second Story Press, Toronto, 1994.

The Shared Heart: Portraits and Stories Celebrating Lesbian, Gay, and Bisexual Young People; Adam Mastoon, photographer; William Morrow, New York, 1997.

The Shelter of Each Other, Mary Pipher; G. P. Putnam's Sons, New York, 1996.

Singing at the Top of Our Lungs: Women, Love and Creativity, Jo-Anne Krestan and Claudia Bepko; HarperCollins, New York, 1993.

Susan B. Anthony Slept Here: A Guide to American Women's Landmarks, Lynn Sherr and Jurate Kazickas; Times Books, New York, 1994.

Teenage Health Care, Gail Slap and Martha Jablow; Pocket Books, New York, 1994.

Things Will Be Different for My Daughter: A Practical Guide to Building Her Self-Esteem and Self-Reliance, Mindy Bingham and Sandy Stryker; Penguin, New York, 1995.

Totally Private & Personal: Journaling Ideas for Girls and Young Women, Jessica Wilber; Free Spirit Publishing, Minneapolis, 1996.

Understanding Your Teenager's Depression, Kathleen McCoy; Perigee, New York, 1994.

The Way We Never Were: American Families and the Nostalgia Trap, Stephanie Coontz; Basic, New York, 1992.

The Wellness Center's Spa at Home, Kalia Doner and Margaret Doner; L.M.T.; Berkley, New York, 1997.

The 1998 What Color Is Your Parachute: A Practical Manual for Job-Hunters and Career Changers, Richard Nelson Bolles; Ten Speed Press, Berkeley, CA, 1997.

Where She Came From: A Daughter's Search for Her Mother's History, Helen Epstein; Little Brown, Boston, 1997.

Where the Girls Are: Growing Up Female with the Mass Media, Susan J. Douglas; Random House, New York, 1995.

Wilma Unlimited: How Wilma Rudolph Became the World's Fastest Woman, Kathleen Krull; Harcourt Brace, New York, 1996.

Women and Numbers: Lives of Women Mathematicians, Teri Perl; Wide World Publishing/Tetra, San Carlo, CA, 1993.

Women and Work: In Their Own Words, Maureen Michaelson; Newsage Press, Troutdale, OR, 1994.

Women, Girls and Psychotherapy: Reframing Resistance, Carol Gilligan, Annie Rogers, and Deborah Tolman; Haworth Press, New York, 1991.

Women in Sports: The Complete Book on the World's Greatest Female Athletes, Joe Layden; General Publishing Group, Los Angeles, 1997.

Women's Bodies, Women's Wisdom, Christiane Northrup; Bantam Books, New York, 1994.

Working Father: New Strategies for Balancing Work and Family, James A. Levine and Todd Pittinsky; Addison-Wesley, Reading, MA, 1997.

Writing a Woman's Life, Carolyn Heilbrun; Ballantine Books, New York, 1988.

Hot Lines

Alcohol: 1-800-356-9996 (see Alanon-Alateen)
Drugs and Alcohol: 1-800-DRUG HELP (1-800-378-4435)
National Child Abuse Hotline: 1-800-422-4453
National Organization for Pregnant and Parenting Teens: 1-301-913-0378
Youth Crisis and Runaway Hotline: 1-800-HIT-HOME

Web Sites

ABL: http://www.ableague.com

Canadian Volleyball League: http://www.iust.women.com

CNN/SI, Women's Sports: http://www.cnnsi.com/womens/

ESPN Sports Zone, Women's Professional Basketball: http://espnet.sportzone.com/wpb/

Feminist.com: http://www.feminist.com

Girl's Club: http://www.worldkids.net/clubs/csis/

Girl's Place: http://www.girlsplace.com/

Girl's Power: http://www.girlpower.com

Girl's Power: http://www.health.org/gpower/girlarea/index.htm

Girl Talk: http://www.livezone.com/girltalk/

Girl Tech: http://www.girltech.com/

A Girl's World: http://www.agirlsworld.com

LPGA Tour: http://tour.golf.com/tour/lpga

Planet Girl: http://www.planetgirl.com/

Surfing-Sufergirl magazine: http://www.surfergirl.com

The WNBA: http://www.wnba.com

Women in the Olympics: http://www.feminist.org/other/olympics/intro.html

Women's Educational Equity Act Resource Center: http://www.edc.org.womensequity/index.html

Women's Hockey: http://www.whockey.com

Women's Soccer Federation: http://www.cris.com/~jg189/wsf/

Women's Sports Foundation index: http://www.lifetimetv.com/WoSport/index.htm

On-Line Magazines

blue jean magazine, 888-4-BLU-JEAN; (web site) http://www.bluejean-mag.com; (e-mail) info@bluejeanmag.com.

Empowered magazine, 888-TEENMAG; from Phoenix area 777-1892; (web site) http://www.eyf.com.

Teen Voices, 888-882-TEEN; (web site) http://www.teenvoices.com; (e-mail) womenexp@teenvoices.com.

HUES, 800-HUES-4U2; (web site) http://www.hues.net; (e-mail) hues@hues.net.

New Moon, 800-381-4743; (web site) http://www.newmoon.org; (e-mail) newmoon@newmoon.duluth.mn.us.

New Moon Network: For Adults Who Care About Girls, 800-381-4743; fax 218-728-0314.

Girls, Young Women, and Leadership

Take Our Daughters to Work day is only one part of the Ms. Foundation's efforts to address the needs and concerns of girls and young women.

The Ms. Foundation for Women launched the Girls, Young Women, and Leadership Program (formerly the National Girls' Initiative) in 1991. In the Collaborative for Healthy Girls/Healthy Women, some of our more than twenty partners include the Charles Stewart Mott Foundation, the John D. and Catherine T. MacArthur Foundation, the Moriah Fund, Ortho-McNeil Pharmaceutical, and Procter & Gamble. Partners bring varying perspectives from their experience as national, local, and women's funds, as well as individual donors.

As we know from experience and research that you've read about in this book, girls are resilient before adolescence but then experience a drop in self-esteem. In addition, many girls experience poverty, discrimination, sexual abuse, and intense depression. Yet we know that girls have strengths and capacities that are valuable for their healthy transition into womanhood and for their leadership in larger communities.

The goal of each component of this program is to help prevent problems *before* they take root, by making girls' developmental issues widely known and understood, and by generating support for programs through which girls stay healthy, strong, and resilient.

The Goals of the Girls, Young Women, and Leadership Program

- To study, document, and disseminate how girls are faring—emotionally, physically, academically, and economically—at school and home and in their communities.
- To educate all Americans about the needs of girls, using direct action, meetings and conferences, popular and scholarly books and reports, polls, surveys, and the Internet.
- To support—financially and with information and technical assistance—grassroots and national nonprofit and academic organizations in which girls develop leadership skills and promote well-being as an integrated endeavor.
- To convene, network, and collaborate with organizations working in girls' interests.
- To provide parents, community-based organizations, educators, and the private sector with practical advice on how they can work with and learn from girls.
- To advocate with and on behalf of girls in all areas of decision-making.

Some of the Projects of the Girls, Young Women, and Leadership Program

- **Annual Grants to Girl-Focused Organizations.** Every year the Foundation helps girls to change their lives and communities by directing resources to grassroots organizations that work on girls' health, violence against girls, gender role stereotyping of girls, nonsexist and nonviolent curricula, teen pregnancy, and self-confidence and vitality of adolescent girls.

■ **Body Politic: Transforming Adolescent Girls' Health.** In January 1996, the Foundation published this report on the findings of the Healthy Girls/Healthy Women Roundtable. In March 1994, the Roundtable convened more than thirty researchers and practitioners from the fields of medicine, psychology, developmental psychopathology, education, and girls' programming to share research and practices that keep girls healthy from childhood through their transition into womanhood.

■ **Programmed Neglect: Not Seen, Not Heard.** In 1993, the Foundation published this report in response to a survey that indicates that less than 8% of all programs nationwide provide services to girls between the ages of nine and fifteen. This report discussed the lack of programming aimed specifically at girls and the problems girls face living in a violent and sexist world. *Programmed Neglect* outlines the kinds of programs girls need, and highlights some of the best programs that are helping girls grapple with the complexities of their lives.

■ **Collaborative Fund for Healthy Girls/Healthy Women.** The Foundation established a Collaborative Fund for Healthy Girls/Healthy Women, a joint effort among foundations, corporations, and individuals. The Healthy Girls/Healthy Women Collaborative directs resources to programs for girls that provide opportunities to conduct research, learn how to make a difference in their communities and develop their capacities for leadership, research, public policy, and grant-making on behalf of girls. This Collaborative focuses on the health, strength, and resiliency of girls and builds the capacity of projects that have the most potential for supporting girls in changing their lives and communities. In September 1997, the Foundation awarded grants to fourteen model girls' programs, and is engaging these grantees in innovative participatory, evaluation, leadership development, and capacity-building activities, using technology and networking. The programs are:

After School Action Programs
  Chicago, IL
AIDS and Adolescent Network of New York
  New York, NY
Asian Pacific Environmental Network
  Oakland, CA

Asians and Pacific Islanders for Reproductive Health
    Oakland, CA
Center for Anti-Violence Education
    Brooklyn, NY
Center for Young Women's Development
    San Francisco, CA
Cool Girls
    Atlanta, GA
Mi Casa Resource Center for Women
    Denver, CO
Native Action
    Lame Deer, MT
Research for Action
    Philadelphia, PA
Sisters in Portland Impacting Real Issues Together (SPIRIT)
    Portland, OR
Step by Step
    Harts, WV
White Buffalo Calf Women Society
    Mission, SD
Young Women's Project
    Washington, D.C.

For more information, contact the Ms. Foundation for Women at 212-742-2300.

How to Get Involved

Take Our Daughters to Work day is always on the fourth Thursday in April. It's never too early to start planning! You can get great information to help you plan the Day—for yourself, for your daughter, for your workplace—from the Ms. Foundation for Women.

Literature like the Organizer's Kit, the Parents Guide, the Guide for Girl Organizers, and more can be ordered anytime during the year.

You can also order official Take Our Daughters to Work day T-shirts, buttons, stickers, trading cards, backpacks, and more.

Here's how you do it:

Call 800-676-7780 to place your order or to get an order form showing you all the literature and merchandise. You can fax your order to: 919-331-1728 or mail it to **Ms. Foundation for Women,** P.O. Box 890350, Charlotte, NC 28289-0350. And if you want another option, check us out on the web at http://www.ms.foundation.org. You'll see the order form on our web site—and place your order then!

The next few pages include some of the information and activities from the organizing literature. *Enjoy!*

Now, for the basics:

Who can take girls to work?

All of us. Any caring adult can take a daughter or daughter-for-a-day to work! Parents, friends, aunts, uncles, cousins . . . mentors and mentors-to-be in addition to family. It's not mother-daughter day, it's Take Our Daughters to Work day. And don't forget, *our daughters* means *all girls!* Some girls go to work with adults whose jobs look like what *they* might want to do. Other girls go to work to learn about jobs they don't know about yet.

What girls can go to work?

Take Our Daughters to Work day is recommended for girls aged nine to fifteen. You learned a lot about what can happen to girls during this period. But girls younger than nine and older than fifteen can really benefit from a lot of the things in this book.

How many people participate in Take Our Daughters to Work day?

Millions of people have participated since Take Our Daughters to Work day was created in 1993. According to a 1997 Roper Starch Worldwide poll, 48.3 million adults said their company or their spouse's company participated in the Day. That means a lot of girls have gone to work . . . and millions more will!

Grown-ups How-To Sheet

Girls are the next generation of women who will work in the world and change the world. What will that be like? Imagine a day when girls are working absolutely everywhere, in boardrooms, city halls, union halls, and concert halls. Imagine a day when girls speak their minds and adults listen respectfully to their opinions and ideas. Imagine a day when boys in classrooms talk seriously with one another about girls and women. Imagine a day when teenage girls are as sure of themselves as when they were eight or nine, a day when girls realize they're not too smart, too tall, too fat or too shy. Imagine a day when girls think they're just right.

Every April, on the fourth Thursday of the month, millions of girls across America participate in Take Our Daughters to Work day with parents, teachers, and employers. The Ms. Foundation for Women de-signed this national event to focus on girls' ideas, needs, and dreams and to help ensure that girls remain confident, strong, and in school throughout their teen years.

Participation is easy. The first thing you need to do is ask the girl in your life—your daughter, granddaughter, niece, neighbor, or friend— if she wants to go to work with you (maybe she has a friend who'd like to come along, too). Find out if she wants to see where you work, interview your co-workers, learn about the different jobs women do, or try her hand at something new. Then give her a copy of the Girls How-To Sheet to help her prepare. If you can't take her to work, find an adult who can—maybe your carpool mate or your sister-in-law. If you're a homemaker or run a home-based business, plan a day in which girls can help out.

Let your co-workers, employees, and boss know you plan to bring a girl to work, and see if your workplace will sponsor a group of girls who otherwise might not be able to participate—girls from an area school, housing complex, homeless shelter, Girl Scout troop, YWCA, or Big Sisters group. Recommend that your workplace send for the Organizer's Kit, which explains how to coordinate the Day with the media, schools, and others in your local community.

Talk to school officials about the Day. Inform teachers, principals, PTAs, and superintendents that you plan to bring a girl to work with you or that your workplace plans to host a group of girls. Recommend that schools purchase the Working It Out lesson plans to prepare students for Take Our Daughters to Work day and to explore related topics with girls and boys throughout the year.

Remember, you will be among millions of Americans demonstrating their support and concern for girls and making girls' dreams mean business on the fourth Thursday in April.

Grown-ups Checklist

What to Do at Home

- Ask your daughter, niece, or young friend if she'd like to go to work with you. See if she has any friends who are in need of a workplace to visit for the day.

- Give her a copy of the Girls' How-To Sheet.
- Talk with her about what she wants to do when she gets older and tell her what you had to do to prepare for the job you have today.
- Get a copy of the Parents Guide, which explains how to prepare for the day, as well as ways to support girls throughout the year.
- Tell your neighbors and friends about Take Our Daughters to Work day. Give them copies of this sheet and encourage their participation.
- Send an announcement about the day to the calendar listing or "events around town" section of your local newspaper.
- Get a copy of the Outreach Guide and learn how to take a leadership role in organizing the day for girls and businesses in your community.

What to Do at Work

- Tell your boss, co-workers, and employees about Take Our Daughters to Work day.
- Distribute copies of the Grown-ups' Sheet at your workplace.
- Get a copy of the Employers Guide, which not only explains why Take Our Daughters to Work makes good business sense, but also answers commonly asked questions and provides sample schedules and activities to try with girls.
- Encourage your boss to form a Take Our Daughters to Work committee and to host a group of girls for the day.

What to Do with Local Schools

- Talk to school officials about Take Our Daughters to Work; give copies of the Grown-ups' Sheet to teachers, principals, and the local school superintendent.
- Suggest they get a copy of the School Guide, which explains how to join with local businesses, arrange for transportation and excused absences, and create gender-equitable classrooms for girls and boys.

- Tell your PTA about the day and distribute the Grown-ups' Sheet at the next meeting. Encourage them to review Facts on Women and Girls and to get involved in planning!
- Volunteer to work with teachers taking groups of girls to work.

Girls' How-To Sheet

You are the next generation of women who will work in the world and change the world! What will that be like? Imagine a day when girls like you are working absolutely everywhere, conducting orchestras, legislating law, designing furniture, delivering babies, rousing audiences, fighting fires, piloting planes, researching whales, exploring the solar system, welding, fishing, judging, singing, inventing, you name it. Imagine a day when adults, including your parents and teachers, listen respectfully to your opinions. Imagine a day when no question is too stupid to be asked and when you'll get an answer. Imagine a day when the boys in your class talk seriously about girls and women, and that on this day you're not too smart, too tall, too fat, too loud, or too shy. Imagine a day when you're just right and the world opens its doors to you.

Every April, on the fourth Thursday of the month, millions of girls ages nine to fifteen, parents, guardians, and teachers participate in Take Our Daughters to Work day, a national event devoted to your ideas, spirit, and dreams. It's a day when you go to work instead of school. You'll have a chance to meet doctors, garment workers, zookeepers, and DJs and talk to them about their jobs. It's a day when you'll be able to tell the president of a company why you would or wouldn't want to work there.

Participating in Take Our Daughters to Work day is easy. The first thing you need to do is tell your parents or guardian that a great thing is happening on the fourth Thursday in April, and see if you can go to work with one of them for the day or with your grandfather, aunt, sister, cousin, next-door neighbor, or friend.

Or . . . organize Take Our Daughters to Work day yourself with your friends and classmates! Where do you and your girlfriends imagine yourselves working in ten or fifteen years? Write or call the mayor's office, a nearby animal clinic, or a local newspaper—wherever you want to learn about what it takes to be a grown-up on the job. Ask if they'd be willing to sponsor you or all the girls in your grade on Take Our Daughters to Work day.

Once you know where you'll be working, start asking questions! What will your job be during the day? What should you wear and where will you eat lunch? Get a special notebook to take along on the job, and write down your questions, ideas, and feelings. On Take Our Daughters to Work day, think of yourself as a welcome reporter. See for yourself the different kinds of jobs women do. Ask lots of questions. Try your hands at something new. But most important of all, have fun!

Ms. Foundation for Women
120 Wall Street, 33rd floor
New York, NY 10005
800-676-7780

To order organizing material like the Organizers' Kit, Parents Guide, Employers' Guide, and School Guide, and don't forget the Guide for Girl Organizers, call 800-676-7780. You can also order T-shirts, buttons, stickers, and more!

Girls' Checklist

Here's how I can get ready for Take Our Daughters to Work day

At Home:

- Ask a grown-up to take me to work on Take Our Daughters to Work day or to help me get in touch with a place that my friends and I would like to visit.
- Tell her/him to get a copy of the Grown-ups' Sheet, which explains how it all works.
- Ask my mom, dad, or guardian to get the Parents Guide and give me the Interviewing the World and Girls at Work handouts. These will help me get ready for the big day.

- Get a special notebook and write down questions I want to ask people on the job.
- Write a list of twenty things I like to do (e.g., solve equations, play soccer, laugh, give good advice) in my notebook.
- Decorate the cover of my notebook to look like me: my personality, interests, and dreams.
- Interview a grown-up I like about her work.

At School:

- Tell my teacher and principal I want to go to work on the fourth Thursday in April.
- Suggest that they get copies of the Grown-ups' Sheet and School Guide, which explain what Take Our Daughters to Work day is all about.
- Work hard on the special Working It Out activities that help prepare my classmates and me for the Day.

With My Friends:

- Find out where my girlfriends from school, clubs, and my neighborhood or housing complex will be working.
- If some of my friends don't have a workplace to visit on Take Our Daughters to Work day, see if they can come along with me.
- Write a letter to a local business or organization—maybe a radio station, courthouse, hospital, or construction company. Tell them we're interested in their work, and ask if they'd host a group of girls on Take Our Daughters to Work day, the fourth Thursday in April. Suggest that they get the Employers Guide, which explains what the day is about and how to plan for it.
- Read parts of the Parents Guide to find out why the day has been created especially for girls, and what boys will be doing while we're at work.
- Share my special notebook, ideas, questions, and dreams about work with my friends.

Fill in the blanks:

I would love to be a _____ when I grow up.
(your dream job goes here: e.g., veterinarian, inventor, dancer)

I am going to _____ on Take Our Daughters to Work
day.   (name of adult's workplace)

At the Workplace

If you're organizing Take Our Daughters to Work day at your work-place, you might want to order the Employers Guide, which includes tips, activities, and common questions. You also can order our newest publication, *Bright Ideas: Helpful Ideas, Successful Activities, and Useful Forms.*

Here's some information based on the Employers Guide to get you started:

So you're a little daunted by the prospect of integrating two or three or, in some cases, three dozen twelve-year-olds into your workday? Well, previous participants will tell you that the whole process is really rather easy. People visit your organization all the time—for meetings, interviews, conferences. The only difference on Take Our Daughters to Work day is that your visitors will be younger—and maybe a bit more curious and energetic.

Here are some basic guidelines to get you started:

Set up a Take Our Daughters to Work day Organizing Commit-tee. Perhaps you'll be coordinating with local authorities to spon-sor a group of "daughters" from a neighboring school or housing complex. In other cases, girls will spend the day with their parents or adult hosts. Whatever the situation, it's a good idea to assemble a committee that can be charged with determining a schedule and orchestrating activities for girls. Why not include girls who will be participating in the Day on your committee? The day will work best if the CEO or head of your organization takes an active role in designating someone to lead the committee. Round out the committee with the adult hosts—parents, aunts, uncles, grandmothers, family friends—and other employees who are proud of and eager to present the work of your organization.

Tap Into Your Existing Resources. Your organization no doubt has a routine for initiating new recruits. With minor modifications, this routine should work well for Take Our Daughters to Work day. (Draw, as well, from the suggested activities in this guide.)

Take Advantage of Your Own Knowledge and Experience. It may well be twenty years that you've owned your small business, or it may seem a lifetime that you've been troubleshooting at a computer firm, and perhaps you are wondering what in your day's work could possibly be of interest to a girl. For a ten-year-old, it's unlikely that *any* part of your experience will be boring; the most routine tasks—sending a fax, booking a trip, talking with a supervisor—are new and noteworthy. Girls will be interested in your business itself, the ins and outs of how things happen and how the various parts of an organization work together. Girls will also be curious about people, how they relate, and what happens when they disagree. Girls will want to know about you, too, what you do, and the education and training that prepared you for your job. They'll wonder about your dreams when you were their age. Who were your role models? What are your goals now? How do you combine your job with raising children and other outside interests?

You—and every employee—stand to be a mentor to girls. So on Take Our Daughters to Work day, all the people girls meet should be prepared to explain what they do, how they got there, and why their work is meaningful. This includes not only CEOs and department heads but particularly entry-level workers, because they're the ones with the jobs in which girls can begin to envision themselves. Girls want honest answers about what works and what doesn't. Just remember to speak in language geared to kids. Hearing directly from you and the people at your organization will prepare girls for—and excite them about—what lies ahead.

Alert Your Community to This Innovative Campaign. In advance of the day, contact the school system in your area (school boards, the superintendent, principals), the chamber of commerce, public housing authorities, and the local media. Announce your involvement in a press release.

Be Creative! Nobody knows your workplace better than you do, so you know better than anyone what might fascinate girls. But resist the temptation to overplan; we convened meetings with participants from all kinds of organizations who couldn't stress this enough. Let girls' curiosity drive the day.

Here are some helpful hints and a form from *Bright Ideas: Helpful Ideas, Successful Activities, and Useful Forms*:

Helpful Hints in Planning Activities

- Structured activities usually are scheduled in the morning, with one-on-one activities in the afternoon.
- Use thirty to forty-five minutes at the end of the day for evaluation and debriefing.
- Use interactive activities and games relating to the organization to enhance the learning.
- Presentations are aimed at specific age groups, with eight-to-eleven, twelve-to-fourteen, and fifteen-and-up being the most popular groupings.
- Have cultural arts programs during lunch with girls participating—singing, dancing, playing simple musical instruments such as bells.
- Have the girls develop, working in teams, a workplace-related plan, product, forecast, etc.
- Develop a series of handouts about the organization that the girls can share with their families, classmates, and others.

Sample School Excuse Form
(Please adapt as needed)

(LETTERHEAD)

On April (date), (year) _____ (company) _____ and its employees will participate in the annual Take Our Daughters to Work day, sponsored by the Ms. Foundation for Women. _____ (company) _____ and its employees invite their daughters, relatives, friends, and other sponsored girls between the ages of _____ and _____ to attend. The girls will be participating in interactive learning activities that will lead toward their getting a better grasp of the world of work and the skills needed to be hired in specific professions.

It is the intent that the employees of _____ (company) _____ will serve as role models and will inspire the girls to strive to attain their full potential. Also, the girls will be shown how such courses as science, math, and business can better prepare them for a wide variety of jobs unheard of to previous generations of girls.

Parent/Guardian/Sponsor, please fill out the bottom of this form and have the girl take it to her teacher or principal to sign. You may keep the paper, or it can remain at the school.

Parent or Guardian or Sponsor's Name _____

Teacher _____

School _____

Student's Name _____

I excuse ___(student's name)___ to attend the Take Our Daughters to Work day, April (date), (year). If necessary, the student should complete the following work to make up for the excused absence.

_____

_____

Signature _____ Date _____

(teacher or principal)

This is a work interview form. You can also use these questions as a starting point for discussions about work:

Company _____ Date _____

Person Interviewed _____ Position _____

Type of Work or Business _____

1. At what time do you come to work? _____

2. At what time do you leave work? _____

3. How many hours a week do you work? _____

4. What are your most important duties? _____

_____

_____

5. What are the hardest things about your job? _____

_____

_____

6. What are the best things about your job? _____

_____

_____

7. What is the worst thing that has happened on your job? _____

_____

_____

8. What special education or training does someone need to hold a job like yours? _____

_____

_____

9. What are some other jobs that someone with your skills could perform? _____

_____

_____

---

10. How will your job be different in ten or twenty years? _____

_____

_____

11. If you were preparing to begin your work career again, what would you change? _____

_____

_____

12. What are the most important skills it takes to do your job well? _____

_____

_____

13. What are the duties of your boss? _____

_____

_____

14. What are some things girls should consider when applying for a job? _____

_____

_____

15. My thoughts about this job are _____

_____

_____

For more information about the Ms. Foundation for
Women and Take Our Daughters to Work® Day (the fourth
Thursday of every April), please write us at:

Attn: Girls Seen and Heard
Ms. Foundation for Women
120 Wall Street, 33rd Floor
New York, NY 10005

or call us at:
(800) 676-7780

or e-mail us at:
info@ms.foundation.org

or visit us on the Web at:
http://www.ms.foundation.org

About the Authors

The Ms. Foundation for Women, the country's only multi-issue women's foundation, has been creating opportunities for women for twenty-five years. The Foundation works to improve the lives of women and girls by conducting advocacy and public-education campaigns, providing technical assistance, and directing resources to organizations in the areas of Women's Economic Security; Women's Health and Safety; and Girls, Young Women, and Leadership.

Sondra Forsyth holds an M.A. from Harvard University and has a dual career in publishing and dance. Currently a contributing editor at *Mademoiselle*, she is the author of several books and is a member of the ballet faculty at STEPS on Broadway.